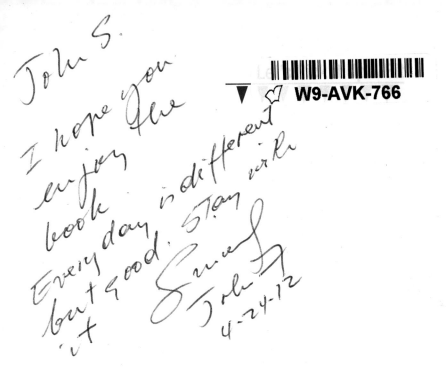

John S.

I hope you
enjoy the
book.
Every day is different
but good. Stay in it

Sincerely
John
4-24-12

▼▼▼

Let's Pick It Up A Bit

John Farah
Nelson Williams

with

Christopher Farah

Thompson Shore, Inc. ▼ Dexter, Michigan

Copyright © 2012 by Let's Pick It Up a Bit, LLC
ISBN: 978-0-9849910-0-6

Book and cover design by Mary Cronin
Illustrations by William Kliber

To my parents, Naim and Marie Farah, whose unrelenting dedication, sacrifices, love and support have shaped my life from childhood to the present. Their work ethic, fairness towards people from all walks of life and honesty are the standards that I try to emulate daily. I feel very fortunate for their guidance over the years. Through their example they instilled in all six of their children the confidence, determination and independence that we each exhibit in our daily lives.

▼▼▼

Contents

I overheard the three runners talking right when I hit the eight and a half mile mark of the race. They were young, in their twenties. They were on the tall side, slim and fit. They sported crew cuts, and they had good running form. They were talking about me.

"We can't let this guy get past us," they said.

It was a challenge, but I didn't need them to get up for the Bobby Crim. The year was 1992, and the Crim was—as it is now—one of Michigan's premiere road races, founded in 1977 by the state speaker of the house, who gave the race his name. The Crim took place in the city of Flint, where my parents and my brother and sisters lived, and my kids had come along to cheer me on. That morning, before the race, my mother had made her special, sweet Arabic coffee—"Ahway Arabiya"—for me and my buddy Nelson, who took a sip, smiled approvingly, and dubbed it "high-octane stuff." Nelson had a knack for witty comments. At 5'5", he was three inches shorter than me, and at 140 pounds a little meatier than my wiry, 125-pound frame. I always thought I was bald—until I met Nelson. But somehow he managed to have even less hair than I did. He was one of my best friends, and my earliest most reliable running partner.

At 7:15 A.M., we drove down to the starting line. Even though we were forty-five minutes early, there was already a festive, carnival atmosphere. Runners were picking up their numbers, starting to cluster in groups of friends or warming up with quick wind sprints down Saginaw Street. They came from all over the country for this race, and Flint did its best to put on a good show—fixing the roads and sealing any pot holes left over from the harsh winter. The city had passed its peak long ago, but it still had its pride.

So did we. The weather was sixty degrees and a bit humid, but that wasn't bad for an August morning, and Nelson and I felt good. I took my shirt off and all I had left were black running shorts with my number folded and pinned neatly to the front. We lined up three or four deep at the start line so we wouldn't get stuck behind slower runners. We were surrounded by guys in their twenties and thirties, slim, fit and eager to dart off at the gun. But we weren't intimidated. This was my tenth Crim, Nelson's first, and we had been training for months. We had a plan of attack, and we were ready.

And for the first several miles, we were right on target. We were shooting for a pace of 6:15 a mile. We did the first mile in 6:07—a little fast, but not too off. "One for the books," Nelson said, pleased with the start. We hit 6:13 in the second mile, 6:25 in the third when we reached a hilly part of the course, then pushed it back down to 6:15. The Bradley Hills—a series of three hills I always dreaded—gave us a little trouble in miles five and six, but we still managed a pace of 6:28 a mile, and we rocketed back to a 6:08 in mile seven, helped on by the cheers of my sister Gisele and brother-in-law George in front of their home. My two sons even made it down for a few minutes, even though at sixteen and thirteen years old they were probably more interested in sleeping than watching runners. The race was a big draw, and crowds of people lined the roads, shouting us on and handing us cups of water to splash over our sweaty heads to cool off. Nelson called out the time from his digital watch every time we passed a mile marker—this was well before the luxury of electronic timing chips. He was usually more talkative, but he was in the zone, conserving oxygen for his hard-working muscles.

Then we hit mile eight. I saw the blue and white stripe on the pavement marking the distance, and I heard Nelson check his watch next to me. "Six minutes and forty-one seconds," he whispered calmly. 6:41. Twenty-five seconds off pace.

"Are you kidding me?" I loudly replied. The terrain was rolling hills, the sun was beating down and we were breathing hard. But my legs felt good and the hardest part of the course was now long behind us.

"Let's pick it up a bit," I told Nelson, and without waiting for an answer I took off. Before I knew it I was running ahead of Nelson for the first time in the race. I wouldn't see him again until the end.

Moments later I came upon the three young runners. I was forty-nine years old, probably double their age. As I closed in on them, the youngest-looking one cast a sideways glance at me. He had long sideburns and a sparse mustache. That was when he said it: "We can't let this guy pass us."

And then I realized. He hadn't said "We can't let this guy pass us." He had said, "We can't let this old guy pass us."

That was all I needed to hear. I checked my watch—I was already back down to a 6:18 pace, and there was just one mile to go in the race. I didn't say a word.

I would let my legs do the talking.

▼▼▼

People always ask me, "John, how do you do it?" Honestly, it takes me a while to understand what they're referring to. After all, I'm not a professional athlete. I'm a normal guy. I have an amazing wife, two fantastic sons, and three great step-kids. I have lots of good friends who I like having dinner with. I'm a dentist with a practice of my own, and I love what I do. I enjoy working in my garden, and I own two cats that sometimes take shits in my basement, which really bugs the heck out of me. Like I said, I'm a pretty normal guy.

I also have run over 120 marathons over the sixty-eight years of my life, and I continue to run and exercise avidly to this day. Just last year, for example, I ran twelve marathons, and that's not counting all the shorter races I've done as well.

Okay, so I guess that part of my life isn't all that normal.

But just as I've been running more and more later in my life, so has running become a huge phenomenon throughout the whole country. Whether jogging recreationally or running competitively, huge numbers of Americans have taken to the streets. According to *Running USA*, 8.9 million people completed road races in America in 2007, up four percent from the year before. Marathons are a big part of that growth, with MarathonGuide.com reporting that 397 marathons took place in the country in 2009, an increase from 372 marathons in 2008. On a purely anecdotal note, I've seen the races I've run my entire life explode in their participation levels, as more and more casual runners take up racing. In 1983, when I ran my first Boston Marathon—unquestionably the most famous marathon in the world—there were perhaps 5,000 participants; today's Boston Marathon features more than 20,000 annually.

Given that amazing level of interest in running and health, it's not as surprising that people want to know "how I do it." That's what this book is all about.

"It" is a method I've been developing and honing my entire life, sometimes consciously, sometimes instinctively, or as a natural response to my environment and upbringing. In fact, "It" is more than a method. It's even more than running. It's a way of life—or "The Lifestyle," as my son Mike likes to say authoritatively.

In the following pages, I've broken down The Lifestyle into nine broad areas:

- Head Start
- Running to Run
- Marathon Man—Embracing the Challenge
- Friends—and Competitors
- Boston—It's All About Pacing
- Blazing Trails
- Beyond Pain, Beyond Recovery
- Light On My Feet
- The Triumph of Desire Over Reason

I've illustrated each area with some (hopefully) colorful anecdotes, as well as with some specific training tips that I've perfected with my running buddy, Nelson, in "Nelson's Corner."

Of course, The Lifestyle isn't static. The whole point is to stay dynamic. There is no one set of rules or way of doing things that can apply to everyone eternally and without exception. Even for me, The Lifestyle is something I continue to adapt as I grow older to keep myself active and fit and healthy, not just physically but mentally, emotionally and spiritually as well. But hopefully this book will serve as a starting off point for anyone who really does want to know how I do it. I am not claiming to have all the answers—I'm still working a lot of them out myself—but at least we can have some fun asking the questions.

And maybe, just maybe, we can make some of those young people sweat a little harder to beat us at the finish line.

Who knows? Maybe we'll be the ones who win.

▼▼▼

I was still running even with the three young men who had taken it upon themselves to "beat the old guy" in the Bobby Crim. But as I picked up my pace, one of the youngsters was already trailing slightly behind me, and I could hear the other two breathing harder and harder. I was breathing hard too, but as Nelson would say, I had "plenty left in the tank."

We veered off Court Street and onto Fifth, the three of us running neck and neck. With only a half of a mile to go, I cranked up the pace another notch without uttering a word. Soon it was just two of us.

As we made the last turn onto Saginaw Street, the last of my competition was huffing and puffing, his face burning red. He was matching me step for step.

"*Yallah!*" I whispered to myself in Arabic. "Let's go!" I cranked it up and beat him by three steps. My final mile was 6:14, for an overall time of 63:15. A little bit slower than I had hoped, but nevertheless well within striking distance of my 62:30 target time.

The guy I barely edged out at the finish line walked over and congratulated me. He couldn't resist asking my age.

"Forty-nine," I said, smiling.

"No way," he said. "No way." Shaking his head, he went to get his two friends, who apologized for calling me an old guy. I thanked them for their thoughtfulness.

Soon after, I found Nelson, who had finished twenty-three seconds behind me, setting a personal record by over four minutes. He was just as thrilled with his finish as I was with mine—and he got even more excited when I told him the story.

"Way to teach those upstarts a lesson," he said, laughing. I couldn't help but agree.

I still remember the first race I ever ran.

I was twelve years old in the Fall of 1955 when my parents decided to send me away to boarding school. I had a good life in West Jerusalem. I played soccer almost every day on the big grassy field of the local YMCA—a luxury, because all the other fields were just packed dirt. I had dozens of good friends, Christians, Muslims and Jews, from all over the neighborhood of Mamilla, just a short walk from the wall that separated our half of Jerusalem, the Israeli half, from the half controlled by the Jordanians. But we didn't think about those things. We were too busy playing soccer, starting early in the morning and going until late at night, with only a short break for lunch. But as much fun as I was having, the education options were limited for Palestinian Catholics so soon after the War of 1948. Some Catholic schools had closed for lack of students, some just weren't up to par. True, I could have attended Israel's public schools, but my parents wanted me to study religion and be exposed to more languages than Hebrew. And so I had to go north, to Nazareth, to the Terra Sancta School for Boys. It was five hours away, a long way from my friends and family, a long way for a boy.

At six o'clock on a sunny Sunday morning, Mr. Eliahou Kramer, a pharmacist and old friend of my father's, came to our home in his green 1940s Chevrolet to take me and my dad, Naim, to the train station. I had packed several pairs of clothes, including three sweaters and a winter jacket for the cold northern winters. My mother, Marie, had baked me a special treat of my favorite *ka'ek bi-ajwa*, ring-shaped cookies filled with dates. I noticed, even though she tried to hide it, that every so often she would wipe away tears from her cheeks. I squeezed in the Chevy's tight back seat, acting brave and trying not to cry, while my dad sat in the passenger seat. Mr. Kramer started the car and pulled away from the curb. Over sixty years old, he wore dark sunglasses, and had difficulty shifting the stick shift. The car jerked badly every time he shifted gears, but he refused to let my father drive. The trip to the station wasn't far, and the train ride itself took up most of the trip, because Jerusalem is nestled in the mountains of the West Bank. From Haifa, we had a precarious bus ride through the curving hills of the Galilee—our young Palestinian bus driver was thankfully far more skilled behind the wheel than Mr. Kramer—and early that afternoon we finally arrived in Nazareth.

That first day, the priests in charge did their best to distract me from my new reality. They took me on a tour of the dormitory, assigned me my bed, and helped me transfer my belongings to my tiny closet. They handed me a padlock and a key instructing me to lock it at all times to protect my possessions. But my situation quickly hit home. The studies were easily manageable, but I missed my family, I missed my friends, and even though I had many distant relatives in Nazareth they might as well have been strangers. Plus, the food was horrendous. Bad food sounds like a small detail, a cliche from summer camp—until you have to experience it every day of your life. Then you realize how important it is, especially having come from a home where good food was the norm. My mom sent one care package after another to supplement the school's meager rations. I wrote letters in French back home almost every week. My parents knew I was not a complainer by nature, so when I went home for Christmas my dad promised to find me a new school. But I had to finish out the school year at Terra Sancta.

One more semester. One very, very long semester.

That was when I discovered running. It was a surprise, totally unplanned and completely unrehearsed. It just happened. During the first term, I had joined the Boy Scouts to meet new people. I enjoyed being active, of course, and the scouts helped keep my mind off home for a time, but it didn't solve my problems. Then in the second term a Regional Jamboree was planned for all the schools and troops in the Galilee area. The area campground looked like a tent city, bustling with activity, festive and fun. Boys my age were everywhere, setting up tents, building fires, cooking, keeping the area in order. The scoutmasters had planned dozens of events and activities—sports, hiking, and orienteering to just name a few. As for me—well, I was the new guy. I followed the crowd and did what I was instructed to do.

Until one day that all changed. An announcement came over the loud speakers: races were planned on the track, and our troop leader, Eddie Abu Nassar, was looking for volunteers. No one in my troop wanted to run the 200-meter dash, so I stepped forward. I had never run a race before, but I figured it was no different than playing soccer. After all, as a right winger I had to cover quite a bit of territory. There wasn't much time for the troop leader to give me instructions. He told me not to jump the gun, to not go out too fast, and lastly to remember that 200 meters was twice the distance of a soccer field.

I ignored all three of his directives.

There were about fifteen kids at the starting line. I took my shoes off to run barefoot. Some of the kids had "tennis" shoes on, but true running shoes did not exist in those days and even if they had none of us could have afforded them. I lined up near the inside lane and waited for the whistle to sound. All fifteen of us paced back and forth, excited and anxious to get going. The guy with the whistle kept teasing us, shouting "*yalla hadreen!*"—okay, ready!—and then not blowing the whistle. I think he thought he was funny, but we didn't—half the field took off just before the first whistle finally sounded. They called everyone back. The second try was better, but four of us still false started. I was one of them. The third time they got serious, warning that anyone who crossed the line early would be disqualified. Two adults stood on either side of the starting line to make sure no one got a head start.

The whistle sounded. I held back, didn't hear anyone shout "false start," and after what seemed like an eternity finally took off. Within fifty meters I had passed every other kid, and by the time I reached the halfway mark no one was close. I kept running hard but I was slowly losing steam, huffing and puffing harder and harder. There was no doubt I went out too fast, but even though I was slowing down no one was closing in on me much. Everyone else was struggling just like I was. The last thirty to forty meters were very difficult and I started to panic thinking I might not make it. Then I looked behind me to see the other kids dragging back and a couple even walking.

I wasn't more than ten meters away from the finish. Many of the scouts were there, cheering the runners on, and when I won I was mobbed by people congratulating me. It felt good getting to the finish and I was shocked I had won so convincingly—though far from effortlessly. I was still breathing hard when my scout master, Eddie, a little bit on the rotund side, patted me on the back. "I'm surprised how fast you ran," he said. I was going to say so was I but decided to stick with "thank you." Before I could say anything else he added, "I would like you to run the 100 too."

"But I thought Paul Feher was running it," I said.

"You are both running it," he replied. "I think you're faster."

I didn't object because I didn't think I could, and so it was that forty minutes later I was again standing at the starting line with

Paul next to me. Paul was a person I played soccer with, he was a bit older and a grade higher, a nice kid, originally from Yugoslavia, and a good soccer player. I thought I was faster than him on the field, but he was definitely a better and stronger player so I wasn't sure what to expect.

The whistle sounded and we all took off fast. I stayed next to Paul because I knew he was competitive. We were both breathing hard and by the halfway mark we were pulling ahead of the rest of the field. I was surprised I could stay with Paul because I was still pretty tired from my first race. Sure enough, with twenty meters to go, he started pulling ahead of me.

"You can run faster," I said to myself in Arabic. Slowly I closed the gap. With five meters to go I picked it up another notch. "You can run faster, you can run faster!" I repeated it over and over again. At the last moment I passed him, winning by not more than one step. I was amazed. I was delighted. Frankly, I couldn't believe it.

I was swarmed by kids congratulating me. Paul came over and shook my hand. "Nice run," he said, and walked away. I was a celebrity for the rest of the day; it felt good, but most importantly I met many new kids that day. I finally had a circle of friends, one of the things I had missed most from my home in Jerusalem.

Somehow those last few months in Nazareth weren't quite as long as I thought they'd be.

▼▼▼

As magical as that first race was for me, the results didn't happen by magic. True, I wasn't training regularly as I do now, running miles every day by myself or with my friends. But even at that age, my Lifestyle—yes, there's that word again—readied me for

success. The habits instilled in me by my parents and my teachers
—by a childhood in the Middle East, always an adventure—are
what truly gave me my head start.

My parents had unusual upbringings, even for Jerusalem in the
early Twentieth Century. My father, Naim, was born in Nazareth in 1916 and was only two years old when both of his parents died. He was promptly packed onto a donkey and sent off
to a Jerusalem orphanage to be raised with his two brothers and
sisters. The orphanage was run by the Sisters of Charity, an order of French Catholic nuns. It was a massive place, a complex
of stone buildings surrounded by a giant ten-foot-high stone
wall, with a large garden and even its own laundromat. Almost
entirely self-sufficient, and undoubtedly very intimidating for
someone so young. And as fate would have it, it was the same
place my mother, Marie, was also raised. Her mother was a wid-
ow who couldn't afford to raise her three children alone, and so
kept them at the orphanage while she spent her days cooking
and cleaning for the well-to-do.

At the convent a teacher named Pelagie made sure that Marie
and Naim got a basic education and a strong work ethic. Pelagie
was what was back then called, perhaps insensitively, a spinster.
In her mid-forties, with big black eyes and an infectious smile,
she had once been tall and beautiful. Then, as a teenager she
lost most of her left arm in a train accident, eliminating any
chance of her marrying an eligible bachelor. She never became
a nun, but she did move into the convent. She was more than a
teacher, really. This woman who spent her life without a mate of
her own served as my parents' matchmaker. Although my parents lived in the same convent, they had never formally met—
the boys and the girls lived in different wings and the watchful
gaze of the nuns created an imaginary wall between them. But
at the age of twenty-four, Naim wanted to find a good wife for

himself, and Pelagie pointed him toward Marie. Soon after, on October 13, 1940, Marie and Naim married at the Church of the Holy Sepulcher, the traditional site of Christ's death, burial, and resurrection. To no one's surprise, Pelagie served as the maid of honor.

As it happened, the convent of the Sisters of Charity ended up being a dominant force in all of our lives, a bedrock of security during insecure times—from World War II through the 1948 War between Israel and the Arabs and after.

In 1940, World War II was well underway, the tourism industry in Palestine had crashed, and jobs were scarce. Palestine was a British protectorate, in a political limbo with no real national identity of its own. After they married, my parents made their first home just two blocks away from the convent, in an apartment right above Barclay's Bank. The building was made of stone with the kind of red terracotta roof common in that part of the Middle East, and a long steep staircase with a wrought-iron banister—a staircase I tumbled down twice in my eagerness to haul giant, empty tin water containers down the steps. Always trying to show off.

My three sisters and I were born soon after my parents moved in—Gisele in 1941, me in 1943 and Alice and Nellie in 1945 and 1947. But it was another member of our family who became one of our most permanent fixtures of home life: my father's Aunt Rafia, who lived nearby in Jerusalem's Old City. Aunt Rafia was my grandmother's sister on my dad's side, and she liked my mom because my mom would make her a simple Mediterranean lunch of bread, yogurt, olives and sliced tomatoes and cucumbers with a small demitasse of Arabic coffee after. For her part, my mom always credited Aunt Rafia with teaching her how to make that good Arabic coffee, something my aunt considered an art. The secret lies in getting a thick creamy froth on top, what the Arabs call "*ishta*," which discriminating coffee drinkers cherish and covet. The recipe is so good I still use a variation of it myself to make Nelson's infamous "high octane stuff." Just further proof that it's the little early details of life that often go into making a runner great.

"*Biddi at-lakkah*," Aunt Rafia would say after sipping her coffee. "I want to lie down."

My mom would put a spare mattress for her on the living room floor near the window. Aunt Rafia curled up on the mattress, my mom covered her with a wool blanket and it wasn't long before her snoring would permeate the whole apartment. That didn't seem to bother my mom. When Aunt Rafia woke up, she would drink a glass of cold water, give my mom a hug and waddle out the front door. I think my mom loved Aunt Rafia like the grandmother she never knew.

But the church—the convent, really—always provided our family's main support and community. My dad worked nights as a clerk, and my mom liked being so close to the familiar confines of the convent. I think the nuns liked having us nearby as well. We attended church regularly, visited often, and my mom could drop us off there when she needed to run errands. Some of the residents were blind or deaf, still they sensed our arrival, and it always created quite a commotion. It seemed like the minute we entered a bunch of people would grab and lift us in their arms, all the while hugging and kissing us. Mass was a special occasion, because we loved listening to the nuns singing in Latin. My dad would always chime in zestfully when they sang "Tantum Ergo," and my embarrassed mother would whisper, "*Ouskut!*" "Be quiet!"—but he would just sing louder. He loved singing in Latin, because it connected him to his youth. As for me, I had no idea what the words meant, but the music was so soothing I didn't even care.

That all changed in 1947, the year before the War of 1948—but not in the way you'd expect. Instead of being torn apart from the convent by the turmoil, we actually grew even closer. Tension had been increasing within British Mandate Palestine for years as Jews who were persecuted in Europe immigrated and local Arabs felt their position threatened. As troubles came to a head, my dad asked the mother superior, Mother Recamier, if we could move into the compound. She agreed without hesitation. A handful of other families even joined us. I still remember my teenage cousins Basil and George carrying all our furniture piece by piece across the street to the convent—and it's a good thing they did. We thought our stay would last a few weeks at the most, but it ended up being a whole year. Not that fighting raged the entire time, but the lack of security made us afraid. No one knew who was in charge out there. Finally, Israel gained control of what became known as West Jerusalem, and my dad set out immediately to find us a new place.

Surprise, surprise—it ended up being a few blocks away from the convent, a ground-level unit in a building owned by a friend of the nuns named Affifé Lorenzo. Our new home was on Mamila Street, not far from the YMCA. I was seven years old.

▼▼▼

More than any other part of my life, Mamila prepared me for everything I encountered after I left home—for boarding school, and later on, for America. When I think of my childhood, I think of Mamila.

As soon as we moved into our new place, I could see why my parents loved it. Our first-floor apartment looked out onto a quaint courtyard, tucked far back from the busy street. The building was traditionally Middle Eastern, two stories with six units, made of strong old stone. Near the roof, keeping a watchful eye over the entire courtyard, was a statue of the Blessed Virgin Mary. The weathered statue was tucked into a protective stone niche and surrounded by flowering potted plants, carefully tended by Affifé Lorenzo. Mary had a smile on her face, as if saying to my mom, "You're making a good choice, this is where you and your family should live."

Within a few weeks other tenants moved in and the whole place was teeming with a wide assortment of families and individuals of various ethnicities—Bulgarians, Iraqis, Romanians, Germans and Palestinians. The new crowd of people helped us to adjust to our new reality—thanks to the war we were cut off from some of our closest friends and family, like Aunt Rafia, who were stuck on the Jordanian side of Jerusalem. And the courtyard was a perfect spot for us kids to play and meet other friends.

On the second floor and next to Affifé's own apartment was a mixed Muslim-Jewish family, the Awads, with three children: two boys, Yahya and Ghazi, and a daughter named Kawsar. Their Muslim dad, Ali, worked as a driver at the French consulate, and their Jewish mom, Naomi, stayed at home, as did most mothers back then. Yayha was my age and we quickly started getting into all the kinds of mischief seven-year-olds can get into together. Right next to the Awads was a Palestinian Christian couple, Farhan and Marie Ghattas, who didn't have any kids. Next door to us was a Sudanese man, Ahmed, a sketchy character who turned out to be a child molester and was jailed after some neighbors complained to the police. Next to him was a guy by the name of David, mellow and friendly and somewhat effeminate, who I later learned was gay. I noticed that other men often visited him, and when I asked my mom why she just told me he preferred male friends. That was good enough for me.

My mom's favorite neighbors were the Niedermans and Schmidts, who lived in another, bigger building owned by Affifé, and had children our age. Mr. Neiderman had two daughters and was nice to our family from the outset, always visiting to ask if we were okay and in need of anything. The Schmidts had two boys and a girl, and while the dad was a volatile guy who fought a lot with his wife, Shulamit, she was much more laid back. I remember when neighborhood kids would tease me and my sisters for being Palestinian, Shulamit would open her door and say in her mocking, drawn-out Hebrew, "*Az may yesh?*" "So what?"

Affifé Lorenzo was an interesting character in her own right. Her father was French and her mother Palestinian, both deceased. And she hadn't seen her two brothers, who both lived in France, since the beginning of World War II. Although Affifé was probably in her mid-sixties she looked much older as did many of the people of her generation, who had been through so much. She was extremely overweight, probably diabetic, and she walked with a cane because her right leg was easily three times the diameter of her left leg and cylindrical in shape, like a big fat sausage. Her walk was slow and deliberate—and she walked everywhere, especially to Mass, which she attended daily at the convent.

When my mom saw her coming she would always invite her in for cookies and Arabic coffee, a new friend to fill the void left by Aunt Rafia. Affifé and my mom would sit and chat and listen to the BBC on the radio, whereas for my part, I was just fascinated by Affifé's cane. Whenever she wasn't looking, I would stealthily "borrow" it and do my best to imitate her funny gait. Amazingly, though, even when she had her ear right against the radio she somehow always knew what I was up to.

"Hello! Hello! *Wain inta?*" she would call in Arabic. "Where are you? That is the only cane I have—it is not a plaything!" My mom would grab me and yell at me for making trouble, even though I really think it would've been impossible to break that damn cane.

Affifé passed away peacefully in 1960, seated on her favorite couch, surrounded by her two cats and her dog, Medor. My mom had already started taking care of the statue of the Virgin Mary that overlooked the courtyard, as Affifé became too old and weak to climb the twenty-five steps to the roof. Now she took over permanently, dusting the cracked, faded blue enamel of Mary's robe and watering the flowers around her with a (literally) religious fervor. Soon after Affifé died, new neighbors moved into her unit—a Jewish couple named Israel and Ruth. Although Israel himself didn't mind the statue of Mary, Israel's old father was bothered by the Catholic icon peering down at him when he visited his son. Israel asked my mother if he could cover Mary with a white sheet when his dad visited, so he wouldn't have to see the statue.

"Tell your dad when he comes to visit to look down instead of up," my mom replied. "Then he won't see a thing."

That ended that discussion. (Years later, in 1975, when my parents immigrated to America, Israel himself took over caring for the statue of Mary, in my mother's honor. He waters the flowers to this day.)

▼▼▼

In the early 1950s I wasn't yet ten years old, but everything around me was in constant change. We had been forced to move, cut off from many of our friends, and my dad had lost his job. But my parents somehow managed to be positive and have hope through it all. We had our new home, my dad found a new job at nearby King David Hotel, and following in their example, I had made new friends and was ready to explore my new neighborhood, my new world.

Along with Yaha, I set out and quickly made a host of new friends: Gadi and Nathan Manhaim, David Ashkenazi, Nicolas Ghawi, Tony Nacib, Joseph Abusharr, Jacob Nimer and Manuel Khouri, to name a few. As you can tell by their names, we were a motley crew of Arabs and Jews, just like my apartment building. We soon started meeting to play soccer at the nearby YMCA, because Nicolas Ghawi's dad was building superintendent there. For Americans it's perhaps hard to understand how central the YMCA was to life in West Jerusalem at the time. Almost similar to the convent, the "Y" had served as a bulwark of stability during tumultuous times, a place for people of different backgrounds to meet and put aside differences, if only briefly. Even now, with its distinct architecture, its arched stone facade and a tower that overlooks the entire Holy City, it remains one of Jerusalem's most famous buildings.

That's where I grew up. Learned to play soccer. And honed the competitive instinct that helps me be a successful runner today.

Nicolas Ghawi's dad not only gave us near-constant access to the soccer field, but perhaps more important he allowed us to play on the technicallly off-limits front lawn. Even today it's hard to find a big well-maintained lawn to play on in the Middle East. Most soccer fields—like the Y's—consist of hard, packed dirt. Being able to play on real grass was an amazing luxury back then, and thanks to Nicolas' dad we were always able to borrow as many soccer balls as we wanted. We were all pretty poor, but we played soccer like kings.

Best of all, our games occupied prime real estate, right at the front of the Y. Everyone around could watch us play, and that's how we met lots of new kids—and many adults—who came back week after week to join in. On some Saturdays we played for eight hours, going home for a quick lunch and coming back in the afternoon to keep going. When I wasn't playing soccer, I was playing ping pong, tennis, volleyball and swimming.

"*Ma b'teshba'ash min il-luob?*" my mother always asked me in Arabic. "Don't you ever get tired of playing?"

Clearly the answer was "*La'h.*" "No."

That was my universe. During the week, I studied at local Catholic schools, one after another as each of them shut down in the aftermath of the war or failed to live up to my family's expectations. But my real life was lived on that grassy field in front of the Y. I gained confidence, I learned to value my friendships but also how to make decisions on my own. Most of all, I learned how to survive and even thrive in a difficult, constantly changing environment.

I was twelve when my parents decided to send me to boarding school, up north in Nazareth. Leaving everything I had known and built behind for a whole new life. And what turned out to be the first road race I ever ran—the first of hundreds.

But in many ways I was more prepared than I could ever know. Specific, detailed training plans are crucial for any runner— we all know that. You have to run to be a runner. But being a competitor—being successful—is about more than just talent or even hard work. It's about creating a strong foundation that can be built on, about creating an optimal environment to succeed. My childhood did that in ways I wasn't aware of, in ways that continue to pay off today.

I had a hell of a head start.

▼▼▼

▼ NELSON'S CORNER 1 ▼ Your Own Head Start

Usually the Nelson's Corners will be by, well, Nelson. In this case, though, I had some special lessons I wanted to share from my childhood at boarding school, so this one is written by me.

Getting started as a runner is about exercise and training, yes—but it's also about environment. Creating a positive, winning environment for yourself at home and at work will help ensure that your first efforts at running will grow and thrive instead of quickly petering out. Even if you've been running for years, improving your environment will help you get more out of your workouts, no matter how fine tuned they are.

That's why this Nelson's Corner is going to include some tips from some very old friends (and taskmasters) of mine—the Christian Brothers who ran the second boarding school I attended, College des Frères of Jaffa. The head of the school was a Czech monk named Frère Benoit, a short, stocky man with a protruding belly, round face, puffy cheeks, and an air of absolute authority. With his keen eyes staring at us through his thick-rimmed glasses, he scared the hell out of us kids. And pretty much everyone else too.

Of course, when you're young you get out of your body what you put into it, sometimes more. As you age, you have to put in more—and you get less in return. So whenever you feel like slacking off, just imagine Frère Benoit peering down at you with his intense, commanding gaze. If that doesn't motivate you, well, you've got more problems than I can help you with.

The Frère Benoit Plan

1. **Keep your room and office space clean and organized.** You've probably heard that cleanliness is next to godliness. According to Frère Benoit, it was the other way around. Every

morning we had to stand at attention next to our beds as he made his inspection—clothes had to be pressed, shoes polished and fingernails clean. If anyone said a word, he would simply whisper, "Come here." One day when he was late, I stood next to the dormitory door in front of my friends and—doing my best Frère Benoit—said "Come here!" They all laughed—until I felt him grab my ear and pull. He was everywhere!

2. **Make your bed every morning.** When I first arrived at College des Frères, before we did anything else we all had to make our beds. I know, it sounds silly. But if you can't keep where you sleep neat, how can you do anything about the rest of your life?

3. **Follow a strict daily schedule.** Our schedule was rigorous. Classes started at 7:10 A.M. At noon, lunch was served. From 12:50 to 1:30 we played organized sports, after which we returned to class until 4:30. After that we had free time until 6:30, when we all ate dinner. At 8:00 P.M., study hall began and lasted until 10:00, when we all went to bed. The next day we did it all over again.

4. **Mornings are especially important.** Mornings set the tone for the rest of the day. As a sophomore, I was responsible for waking younger students up at 6:00 to get them ready for breakfast by 6:30. As incentive to move quickly, any kid who was ready by 6:15 could join me in the courtyard for simple exercises and calisthenics. To my surprise, the program became so popular that soon most of the school was taking part. Even now mornings are my favorite time to run.

5. **Memory exercises.** I learned the importance of memorization the way you learn anything best—because of an attractive female teacher. Pnina was my big-breasted,

twenty-something Hebrew teacher, and like every boy in class I had a big crush on her, so I worked hard to get her attention—by being a total troublemaker. In return, she made me memorize Bible verses from the Old Testament—ten at a time. One day, when I had failed to memorize a single verse, I stood next to her desk and peered over her shoulder to get a look at the book—and instead got a better one of her mighty cleavage. "I'm sure you've seen something like them before," she said, turning bright red. She promptly tripled my assignment. To this day I credit her and her impressive bosom with my equally impressive memory.

6. **Incentivize.** At dinner time we were divided into tables of fifteen students each, with each table responsible for its own service and clean-up. Tables were graded monthly and rewarded for good behavior, and on days when everyone performed well, we were given a special dessert. It sounds trivial, but even small rewards like that can really help you reach goals and develop good habits.

7. **Stay engaged.** The brothers all had inquisitive minds, regularly reading *Le Figaro* and *Paris Match* to stay in touch with current events. Contrary to popular conception, they did not cloister themselves away but embraced the rest of the world, keeping their intellects very sharp.

8. **Do more than run.** Organize a group of your friends to play some kind of sport for one hour every week. It can be anything—basketball, soccer, touch football, even ping pong. When we weren't studying, we were playing sports. Each year we won our games against rival schools because we practiced every chance we had, really helping us gel as a team. Take charge. If you don't get the games started, no one will.

2 Running to Run

▼ ▼ ▼ ▼ ▼ ▼ ▼

It was 25 years before I ran another race.

A long time, I know. Had I grown up in the United States, maybe I could've had a future in running, competing in high school or maybe even college. But in the Middle East, running competitively wasn't a priority. In fact, it didn't really even exist. And so, after the Scouts Jamboree, I didn't run another race until after I came to America.

Even after I did arrive in the States—in August 1962, fresh out of high school in Israel—running was a hobby, something I did casually with my college buddy, Stan Watson. The thing is, as much as I've grown to enjoy running competitively, races aren't what make me passionate about running. I love to run because, well...because I love to run. For its own sake, because it makes me feel good. Not only is there nothing wrong with running casually, but that's what really brought me to the sport in the first place.

Running just to run.

I had moved to America, once again, for school—a common theme in my life. This time, though, for college. Opportunities for a college education were limited for Palestinians living in Israel, so I moved to Michigan, where I joined my brother-in-law, George, and my sister, Gisele. George had opened a small convenience store in Flint, serving the many auto workers. It wasn't always the safest of environments—George bought his most successful store after the owner was shot and killed in a robbery—but I was from the Middle East, so I figured I could handle it.

To improve my English and take some basic qualifying courses, I started out studying at Flint Community College, which later became Mott. That was where I met Stan, my first running buddy, in the Fall of 1963. The circumstances of our introduction were appropriate enough: I was on my way to challenge one of our teachers about the grade he had given me. The course was Physics, the teacher was aptly named "Professor Buzzard," and grade he had given me was a B. Completely unacceptable.

Stan listened to my mission, took a look at me, and promptly said, "good luck."

Buzzard raised my B to a B+ and said he'd raise it to an A if I pulled an A in the second semester. Stan was suitably impressed. He was even more impressed when I studied my ass off and got the A in the second semester. Stan still likes to tell that story today, and I have to admit—I like to hear him tell it too.

Stan and I both transferred to the University of Michigan the next year. We had a lot in common: we came from big families, we worked hard, we had almost no money, and we both loved to party. I liked to organize things—football games, camping trips, anything I could think of—and Stan was always up for anything. It was really only a matter of time before we started running together.

Stan lived a few blocks away from me, and most days we ran early in the morning, around 6 A.M. We wouldn't go far, usually running for thirty or forty minutes, just enough to relax and get a quick workout—but this was years before jogging was a "thing." If people ran, it was because they were on the track team or about to get mugged. Not for fun.

I would get up a few minutes before six and jog over to his place. It's hard to imagine, but back then I was even more wiry than I am now, with a lean, angular clean-shaven face. Maybe even harder to imagine, I had incredibly thick, black hair—so thick it was hard to comb. Later in the sixties I started growing it out to keep up with the hippies, and added a goatee to boot. My shorts were short, my socks were high, and my shoes were white canvas Converse All Star high tops—the same shoes I wore for tennis and racquetball. No Asics GELs or Nike Airs or bizarre hi-tech sole cushioning systems back then.

Sometimes I'd find Stan stretching awkwardly or doing push-ups. He was taller and thicker than me, with a relaxed, almost gangly way about him—Stan didn't sit down in a chair as much as spread himself out on top of it. But most of the time when I arrived, Stan wasn't even there. In fact, he wasn't even awake. Stan had actually been something of a high school track star in Maine—he lettered all four years and ran a 4:38 mile—although if the meets had been earlier than 9 A.M., I doubt he would've even made JV.

But we weren't in high school anymore. Stan's room was on the second floor and his door was locked, and I had no problem shouting at the crack of dawn for him to get his lazy ass out of bed. If shouting didn't work, I'd throw pebbles at his window, like a scene out of a bad production of Romeo and Juliet.

"What's wrong with you?!" his landlady would yell at me, peaking out the door in her wire-rimmed glasses and disheveled hair. "You'll break my windows!"

"Sorry," I'd say, trying to look as innocent as possible. "Can you please tell Stan I'm waiting for him?"

"What do you think I am, his mother?" she would shout back. Okay, so maybe we weren't that far out of high school. But she'd always go get him—probably so I wouldn't really break a window—and Stan would always appear wearing a guilty smirk on his face. Of course, never saying a word about how late he was.

As early as we started, though, our runs were laid-back, informal affairs. We'd run through campus, with its hodgepodge of buildings—the Law Quad, the Grad Library, the old Waterman Gym—all different styles of architecture, and with very little landscaping and greenery. We talked about school, about work and teachers, about politics and the war in Vietnam. But mostly we talked about girls. The girls we liked, the girls we didn't like. The girls we dreamt of, the girls who gave us nightmares. The girls we dated, the girls we slept with, and the girls who stood us up. Michigan's campus actually had a reputation for its poor selection of co-eds—"nine out of ten women in the Big Ten are good looking, and the tenth one attends U of M," the saying went—but that didn't deter us in the least. Besides, we consoled ourselves, that just meant that Michigan women were smarter.

We even started what we called "Parties Unlimited"—a ragtag company that students could hire to organize and throw parties for them. I was the president, my roommate and fellow engineering student, Heinz Grassl, was the vice president, and Stan, well, he didn't have a title, but he was basically in charge of getting the chicks. Stan was the all-American boy of the sixties. Good looking, the quintessential dreamer, he had this softness about him, this aura of eternal optimism. The guy was a babe magnet, and he didn't have to try. Hell, I don't even know if he was aware of it. I, on the other hand, tried very hard—but with less success. I just hoped for some of Stan's residual overflow.

In my defense, even though it was the sixties and everyone was into peace and free love, most Americans still weren't very accepting of foreigners like me and Heinz, who was German. We were less than a generation removed from World War II and the Korean War, and even if people weren't prejudiced they were simply sheltered. They didn't know what to do with us. Of course, that didn't stop me and Heinz from trying. The campus newspaper published a story about Parties Unlimited—and we dutifully told them our goal was to enhance understanding and communication between foreign and American students. (Well, it was!) We left out the part about the girls.

Stan and I rarely, if ever, exceeded twenty miles per week. We were anomalies. We ran for fun before anyone even realized it was fun to run. Maybe there were a few others. But mostly people would stare at us as we jogged by, puzzled if not suspicious. Possibly even questioning our sanity. We were pioneers. Or maybe everyone was right and we were just plain nuts. Either way, we had a great time.

So by the time I ran my first road race in America, I was already in love with running. In 1978, I had moved to Gainesville, Florida, with my wife, Gretchen, and my two-year-old son, Christopher, to take a teaching and research position at the University of Florida's dental school. My son, Michael, was born soon after.

Florida was different. It felt foreign, somehow, after all my time in Ann Arbor. Gainesville was flat and dull, old, musty and southern, and the afternoons were so hot and humid that you could fry an egg on the lid of a garbage can. There weren't many people around, and I almost never saw anyone else jogging in the neighborhood. Soon after we moved, I was working in the garage when my son Christopher, who must've been a little older than two, came up to me and said, "Dad, where is everybody?"

I looked at him with tears in my eyes and said, "That's an excellent question."

I did, however, keep running. Of course, it wasn't the same without Stan—more than a running buddy, he had really become like a brother to me. But running was still my favorite way to clear my mind, gain some perspective, even if the soles of my shoes did stick to asphalt on those hot Florida days. In a weird way, running felt like one of the few things in my life that still connected me to my home in Michigan.

Then, one day in 1980 I noticed that a colleague of mine, Buddy Clarke, had a pair of running shoes in his office. When I asked him if he was planning on running that day, he told me about a race he was training for. A seven-mile run called the Gator Trot. (I wish it had been the Wolverine Trot, but what are you gonna do?) The race was two weeks away. Did I want to run it?

I thought about my complete lack of training, my complete lack of experience minus a couple quick races when I was a kid, my years of treating running as nothing more than a fun little hobby. Then I thought, What the hell. It'll be fun.

"Sure," I said.

Buddy signed me up the next day.

On a Saturday in early May, I met up with Buddy near the start line. Just like twenty-five years earlier, I had no idea what I was doing. I had never run seven miles consecutively in my life. What was I doing?

Buddy told me he was going for a seven-minute pace, and said I should try to stick with him. For the first half of the race, I did. But then I started losing ground, my legs getting tired and rubbery, my breathing ragged and labored. It was yet another hot, humid Florida morning, and during the last two miles the temperature climbed over 80 degrees. Sweat was pouring off my forehead, my headband was soaked, and bafflingly there was only one water stop along the entire seven-mile course.

Despite it all—and to my absolute amazement—I finished only two minutes behind Buddy, in just forty-eight minutes, for a pace of just under seven minutes a mile. Not only that, but I had finished in the top third out of 300 runners, and fourth in my age group.

The perfectionist that I am, I wanted to do even better. Buddy reminded me that I hadn't even trained. He was laid-back, optimistic. He reminded me a lot of Stan in some ways. With the right training, the right preparation, who knew what I could achieve? I knew I wouldn't wait another twenty-five years for my next race.

▼▼▼

It was hard moving to Florida, being cut off from the life I had worked so hard to build. But no matter what, I still had running. There's something about running, a simplicity, a purity, that makes it stand out from all other sports. You can do it anywhere, in any environment, at a moment's notice, by yourself or with other people. All you need is a decent pair of shoes. Heck, considering the current barefoot-running fad, some people don't even need that.

To this day, one of my favorite things to do whenever I travel— wherever I travel, be it New York, Los Angeles, Europe, South America, or the Middle East—is plot a local course for me to run. It's how I ground myself, how I connect with a new location. Doing a few quick miles, my feet learning the new terrain, my lungs breathing the new air, my eyes taking in the streets, the buildings, the culture.

Perhaps more than any single place, running has become my "home."

▼▼▼

▼ NELSON'S CORNER 2 ▼ Your First 10K: A Light Schedule for Casual Runners and Beginners*

Many people have told me that they don't want to go crazy with running (like they think I am), they just want to run a race or two, have fun, socialize afterwards, and go drink a beer. Not too serious.

This Nelson's Corner is for you: a simple, six-step training schedule that will condition you well enough for a 10K race without requiring a huge time commitment. To some of you it may seem easy or slow, but if you're going to start running— even just for fun—it's important to start the right way and avoid injury and frustration.

Step One: Walking

Don't scoff. Walking is an important way to build your base— and it's even great for experienced runners. Begin with a half- mile a day and work up to three miles a day, four days a week. Once you reach that level, you'll be training approximately four hours a week. This number of hours is important to build en- durance and get your body ready for longer distances.

Step Two: Jogging

Once you're able to walk the three miles a day, start to jog por- tions of this distance, slowly increasing the time you spend run- ning. In approximately four to six weeks, you should be able to jog most of the three miles with very little walking. Remember: run at a pace that you feel you can continue. This may require some experimenting. Speed is not important at this point. En- durance is key.

*See *Nuts and Bolts* for training schedules for 5K and 10K distances at various pace targets.

Step Three: More Walking!

That's right—once you can jog the entire three miles, and I'll guess in about half the time it took you to walk when you first started, add more walking before and after your three-mile jog. Bring your total workout time back to one hour. The goal? To encourage warming up and cooling down before and after a run, essential practices to remain injury free. Do this for two to three weeks, then move on to...

Step Four: More Running!

On one of your four training days, add one mile to the running portion of your workout. Continue to walk before and after to fill up the hour. After two weeks, add another mile of running to that same day—for a total run of five miles.

Important! Before moving on to Step Five, make sure you're comfortable running three days at three miles and one day at five miles, with walking each day to make up the hour. If you're not there yet, stick with Step Four for two more weeks. Start looking for a 10K race that's about six to eight weeks in the future. You're almost there!

Step Five: Moving Up

Add one more mile to your five-mile day to instantly turn it into...your six-mile day! This distance will probably take most of the hour, but remember to warm up and cool down by walking. You can also try warming up with very light jogging. Keep up this schedule for about four weeks. By then, you should be able to do all six miles without walking. Send in your 10K entry!!

Step Six: Race Day

It's finally here, the Big Day. Warm up by walking and jogging for about twenty minutes before you start. Don't get caught up in the excitement and go out with the front-runners! Start in the back and treat the race just like your long training day. Who knows, maybe this experience will leave you wanting more.

And remember, have fun!!

▼▼▼

Marathon Man—
3 Embracing the Challenge
▼ ▼ ▼ ▼ ▼ ▼ ▼

The Gator Trot led to other races—thankfully with far less irritating names—mostly 10Ks. I trained for shorter distances, putting in six to eight miles four or five times a week. The more I trained, the more my times improved. I soon went from a time of forty minutes to just over thirty-seven minutes.

I also soon moved back to Michigan. The Florida experiment had taught me a lot—especially that my home was back north, in Ann Arbor. My family and I moved into a small ranch house that had belonged to an old college friend of mine. The neighborhood was small and safe, and what's more I lived near a buddy, Mike Carter, who also ran. Soon after I started running, I picked up another unlikely friend—an elderly woman who lived on one of my longer country routes, loved to garden and would always give me a glass of water as I jogged by her front yard. She even missed me when I switched courses for a while and missed a few weeks of drink breaks.

"Who knows?" she said. "You could've been hit by a car!"

Yep, it was a far cry from Florida, where I wouldn't even see anyone out on my runs. In Michigan, even the strangers seemed to know I was home. All I needed to do was put on my running shoes and head outdoors and I had a great escape from the pressures of raising a family and trying to start a dental practice in a town already loaded with dentists. In the early 1980s running was gaining popularity as a sport and a hobby. When I was an undergrad, people would make jokes about my skinny legs. Now people looked at me and said "Wow, you must be a runner."

But even I had never really considered running a marathon. Ten kilometers was one thing—but twenty-six miles? My brain could barely process that distance. And though running was becoming more acceptable, marathons were still considered the domain of the elite—something only real die-hards did, not the big bonanzas they are today, when it seems like everyone, no matter what kind of shape they're in, wants to run a marathon.

That makes it all the more appropriate that the reason I ran my first marathon had nothing to do with another runner—but a friend of mine from a sailing club.

I first became interested in the University of Michigan Sailing Club (UMSC) during my initial time in Ann Arbor, in the Fall of 1965. The club had plopped a fifteen-foot sailboat right in the middle of the Diag, the heart of Michigan's campus, and that Sunday the club offered rides to the lake where they sailed, twenty miles from town. The "ride" consisted of a couple beat-up old cars outside the Union, one of which was driven by brash, very loud tomboy named Robin Rotz.

"Going to the Sailing Club?" she shouted.

Stan—who I had convinced to come along—jumped in, and I followed. We were both amazed by what we found. Going to the lake was like going to another world. We drove on bumpy dirt roads, past an old dairy farm covered in peeling white paint and surrounded by a dilapidated wooden fence. The lake itself was relatively small with murky brown water and no real beach to speak of aside from some gravelly black dirt. But for a city kid like myself, it was a real adventure.

The boats were Skipjacks, fifteen feet in length, made of fiberglass with two white sails. That day was sunny and windy—probably twenty miles an hour, with gusts topping that. A perfect fall afternoon for sailing—but kind of nerve-wracking for two novices like me and Stan.

I was paired with a guy named Tom Chen, an experienced sailor who owned his own boat, a high-performance Flying Dutchman. Tom gave me a sixty-second crash course on how to handle a jib, what to do when he tacked—terms I was hearing for the first time. He slapped a bright-orange life jacket over my head, and off we went.

The boat rocked and rolled in the wind, and even though Tom knew what he was doing I very clearly did not. Suddenly a gust of wind hit us and the boat lurched, turning violently.

"Watch the boom!" Tom yelled.

I had no idea what a "boom" was, but I saw the shadow of something flying towards me, so I learned—quick. I ducked my head, just barely missing the aluminum beam that framed the main sail, as Tom pulled on the main "sheet"—or rope—to keep us from capsizing. I breathed a long, deep sigh of relief. That was insane!

Needless to say, soon I was sailing every weekend I could. And loving it. It wasn't long before I was the one teaching people how to avoid decapitation on the lake's choppy waters.

The years went by, and in 1980 it was one of my good friends at the Sailing Club, Diane Navarre, who finally—finally—got me to run a marathon.

Her strategy? She didn't give me any choice.

One day in the Spring of 1981, Diane strode into my new dental office—she was also a patient—and slapped a *Detroit Free Press* down on my desk.

"Here John," she said, smirking. "You like to run—why not a marathon?"

I looked at the paper—it was a training schedule for a first marathon, in honor of the upcoming aptly named Detroit Free Press International Marathon, that autumn.

"I don't know," I said. And I didn't. The training schedule didn't look too demanding—it spanned three months, with higher mileage on Wednesdays and Sundays and lighter mileage the rest of the week—but until that point I had never even considered running the massive distance a marathon demanded. I raised the prospect with Mike Carter, my running buddy, and he wasn't exactly thrilled with the prospect of a twenty-six-mile race either.

But Diane didn't care. She was young, crazy, and she loved to talk—the kind of person who instantly lights up a party. And she loved the idea of running a marathon—as long as someone else was doing it.

"Hey everyone!" she would announce brightly at every party, meeting or informal gathering she went to. "Did you hear that John and Mike are running the Detroit Marathon in October? I know, I can't believe it! Isn't that awesome!?"

And everyone would oooh and ahhh and point and ask questions, and before we knew it Mike and I were running the Detroit Marathon—whether we wanted to or not.

You might think that with all the hype around the marathon—not to mention my earlier experience running races sans preparation—Mike and I would have committed instantly to a solid training regimen. Hell, we even had a newspaper article telling us what to do to get ready, right? Well, you would be absolutely wrong.

We did well in the early going, running distances from five to twelve miles according to the plan in "The Freep." But we quickly lost focus, going back to our shorter, more casual runs. Ultimately the longest distance we ran before the marathon was fifteen miles, and we did that only twice. We were full of the confidence—and ignorance—of youth. We ran all the time, we figured—we were in great shape! What more did we need to do?

A lot, it turned out. What resulted was one of the most hellish—and rewarding—challenges of my life.

Mike and I drove to Windsor, Ontario, early on the Sunday of the race. A truly international race, the Detroit Marathon started in Canada, on the east bank of the Detroit River, then passed underneath the river in the Detroit-Windsor Tunnel.

"The only race with an underwater mile!" the advertisements said.

The excitement at the start-line was palpable. We were downtown, the broad streets still littered from partiers the night before. It was still dark outside, and the weather was crisp, with a slight breeze in the air. A few spectators, a few homeless people—and three-thousand runners, clustered together, about to begin a race that actually spanned two nations. Not bad for a first marathon.

Mike and I made our way to the front and wished each other luck. A couple runners I knew had warned me not to go out too fast. My friend Bill Gregory went as far as to say that the race only started at twenty miles. The start gun went off with a crack. And just like when I was a kid, running my very first race in the Boy Scouts, I forgot it all.

I went out at a 6:30 pace. As ridiculous as that sounds, Mike went out even faster—before long I couldn't even see him anymore—though he was twelve years younger than me. And a 6:30 pace was still thirty seconds slower than what I usually ran for a 10K.

At first I felt great. Better than great—I felt fantastic.

"Why do they make such a fuss about all this?" I thought as I clicked by mile after mile. "This is no big deal at all!"

Then I hit mile sixteen. And my legs slowly but surely fell apart.

It started with a slight tightening—nothing to be too alarmed about, I thought—but the tightening quickly got worse. A lot worse. Add to that an exhaustion that spread from my calves to my thighs to my glutes. By the time I hit mile twenty, it felt like my torso was attached to a block of concrete. I lost all control of my legs, literally had to concentrate on every step I took just to get them to move.

I looked to the sidelines and saw spectators standing, cheering and sipping cups of ice cold beer. "Wow, I could really use one of those," I thought.

My head spun. I couldn't stop thinking about the six miles I had ahead of me. I'd heard about people "hitting the wall"—was I hitting the wall? If so, this was the worst wall in the history of all walls. Why did I do this? What was happening to me? This was so stupid! I would never run a marathon again! I would never run at all again! I might not even walk, ▬▬▬▬▬▬

I even resorted to my native tongue to distract me from the pain. "*Shidd il-himmeh*," I kept muttering. "Strengthen your resolve." It was a futile effort. For the last three miles, the most I could manage was walking interspersed with short, stilted running.

My only consolation? The other runners around me weren't doing much better. Yes, misery does like company.

People were walking, slowly, deliberately, painfully, and I could see the agony in their eyes. One guy tried to massage his right hamstring as he grimaced and groaned. As I stumbled in a daze, I saw Debby K., a woman who had dated my friend Stan

Mendenhall, stagger past me—her legs covered in her own shit. She didn't even care. Not only that, now she was beating me.

Seeing Debby actually gave my legs a small surge of energy—how could I let a woman who had crapped herself beat me? I tried to stay with her as much as I could. The whole area smelled like a Port-a-John, and I felt like I was carrying one, moving my legs was so difficult.

I could now hear the loudspeakers on Belle Isle announcing runners crossing the finish line. Unfortunately, I still had over half a mile to go and all I wanted was to bring this madness to an end.

Debby was still leading me. In fact, she even started picking up the pace. Say what you will about her bowels, that woman was a fighter. The twenty-six-mile marker loomed just ahead. I was so close! Agonizingly close—this was by far the hardest part of the race. Imagine, I had just run twenty-six miles and all I cared about was the final two-tenths.

For a moment, I considered trying to pass Debby. Could I do it? Did I have anything left? But the moment was brief—I just wanted to get this over with. Besides, I honestly didn't know if I could have made it through the last couple miles without her motivating me. I was grateful.

At long last I reached the finish. I've never been so relieved in my life. The sun was shining brightly, the trees dazzling with their fall colors. A huge crowd cheered, waving tiny American and Canadian flags. A volunteer put a medal around my neck, and I thanked her with a faint smile. As for my legs, well, they thanked me. They could also barely move, they were in so much pain.

The last hour was like a nightmare I was finally waking up from. Mike Carter and Debby came over to greet me. It amazed me that Debby was not at all concerned about the state she was in.

She simply was not phased. Within seconds a volunteer came over and directed her to an area where she could hose off.

"That was hell," I told Mike.

He, on the other hand, looked pretty damn pleased with himself. Like me, he had gone out too fast—even faster, actually—but he had much more left in the tank for his last six miles, and he finished seventeen minutes ahead of me. He felt great. Did I mention he was twelve years younger than me?

But the truth is that despite the incredible pain—or maybe even because of it—I was hook on marathons from the very start. The same way my first death-defying experience on a sailboat drew me to sailing even more, there was something about the challenge—the pure insanity—of running 26.2 miles that sucked me in. Not just me, but Mike Carter, Debby, and all the millions of people that now flock to marathons every single year, even if they have no interest in being serious, competitive runners.

There's something about the marathon that has universal appeal, and it lies, I believe, in the completeness, the absoluteness, of the challenge. Running a marathon for the first time is like running through the fire. Running a marathon is about struggle, about testing yourself, about the power of human will over our equally human limitations. Running a marathon is life. Sometimes you beat it, and sometimes it beats you. But as long as you keep moving, in the end you win.

I ended up finishing with a time of 3:31—my quick early miles compensating for my implosion at the end. I calculated that if I had gone out at 7:30 or 7:45 I could've finished at least fifteen minutes earlier. More important, I wouldn't have felt like grim death.

Moments after the finish, I just barely began to recover my energy. To feel human again. And I was elated that I had completed my first marathon. I had never felt better or more accomplished. More alive.

I also swore I would never run one again.

I entered the second Detroit Marathon exactly one year later—and finished with a time of 3:19.

So much for that idea.

▼▼▼

▼ NELSON'S CORNER 3 ▼   Training for Your First Marathon

Running a marathon is an amazing experience—and a huge commitment. You should only attempt this plan if you're already running at least twenty miles a week, or about three hours of running.

In other words, finish Nelson's Corner 2 before you tackle Nelson's Corner 3. These Corners are very logically organized!

This entire plan will take about twenty-one weeks from start to finish. To complete a marathon in under five hours will require averaging about seven to nine hours of running per week. In general, you'll need to gradually increase your daily runs to an hour or more, and add an even longer run on the fifth day.

Here's how to do just that—hopefully with far less pain than I experienced!

(**Note:** Maintain a pace you can hold without walking. If you have to walk, you're running too fast!)

Week One

Run a total of five days, alternate a three-mile day with a four-mile day. On the fifth day, add a long run of seven miles.

Week Two

Increase your four-mile days to five miles. Keep your short days three miles, and your long day seven miles.

Week Three

This week, increase your long run to eight miles. Keep everything else the same.

Week Four

Increase your five mile days to six and alternate between three- and six-mile days. Keep the long run at eight miles.

First Month Summary: You've progressed from about twenty-one miles a week to twenty-five miles a week. Congratulations! How do you feel after your first month of training? As always, you should consult with your doctor if you're feeling any adverse effects.

Tip: Make sure you get enough sleep during this build-up phase. Adding extra miles this quickly can take a lot out of you!

Week Five

From here on out, do one of your shorter daily runs on hilly terrain. So for this week, start with three miles on a hilly course, then do the remainder of your runs like week four.

Week Six

Continue alternating three- and six-mile runs for four days, and increase your long run to nine miles. Remember, one of the three-milers must be hilly!

Week Seven

Up your long run to ten miles, while maintaining the other distances—and the hills!

Week Eight

This week, increase the three miles to four and alternate four-mile runs with your six-milers. One of those four-mile days should still be hilly, and your long run should still be ten miles.

Second Month Summary: Woohoo! In only eight weeks you've increased your mileage from twenty to thirty a week. This is a big step towards realizing your goal of running 26.2 miles.

Week Nine

Do a 10K race this week instead of your long run. It will provide a good assessment of your fitness. Make sure you keep a record of your time—and don't forget to warm up for two miles and cool down for at least one.

Week Ten

Keep the four-mile days and the six-mile days, and increase the long run to twelve miles.

Tip: I find it helpful to do the long runs as "out and back" routes—in other words, six miles in one direction, then turning around and running back on the same path. That way adding one mile just means going out an extra half mile. Crazy, I know—but somehow that feels better in my head!

Week Eleven

Now alternate four-mile runs with seven-mile runs. Drop the long run to ten miles.

Week Twelve

Same as week eleven, but now increase the long run to thirteen miles. (The rule about only increasing your long run every other week applies even more as we get into higher mileages like these.)

Third Month Summary: After twelve weeks of training, you're running thirty-five miles a week—and completing a half-marathon in your long run. You should be feeling stronger and more confident every week.

Week Thirteen

This week increase the four-milers to five-milers, to alternate with the seven-mile days. Keep the long run at thirteen miles.

Week Fourteen

Same daily mileage as week thirteen, but increase the long run to fifteen miles.

Week Fifteen

Increase just one of your seven-mile runs to eight miles, and one of your five-milers to six miles. The run sequence I recommend is five miles, then eight, then six, then seven. Keep the long run at fifteen miles.

Week Sixteen

Maintain the same distances for your first four runs (five, eight, six, seven), and increase your long run to eighteen miles. You have now covered forty-four miles in a week, and are officially a big deal.

Week Seventeen

For days one through four, run the following mileages: five, then three, then six, then four. Decrease the long run to fifteen miles. We're lowering your overall mileage this week to rest your body for the long runs next week.

Week Eighteen

Return to the daily mileage of week sixteen (six, eight, six, seven), and increase the long run to twenty miles.

CONGRATULATIONS!! You're almost ready to tackle the marathon! Your next three weeks will involve "tapering"—lowering your weekly mileage to prepare your body for the big race. Your marathon should be scheduled in week twenty-one.

Week Nineteen

Cut your daily runs back to three miles, then six, then four, then another six. Your long run should be no farther than fifteen miles Leave something in the tank!

Week Twenty – The Week Before the Big Race!

Plan daily runs similar to week nineteen, but make the long run only 10 miles. That's right, just ten miles—those first eighteen weeks were tough on your body, and you need to feel strong for next week!

Week Twenty-One – Race Week!

Jog lightly three to five miles two to three times early in the week to stay loose. Do no running two days before race day. Light stretching is okay. Get plenty of sleep. Eat a good dinner and stay hydrated!

Marathon Tips:

- On race day, line up with the five-hour group. In most marathons there are "pacers." These are experienced runners who will control their pace to hit their targeted time.

- No need to warm up—the first few miles of the race give you plenty of warm-up. Do some light stretching, and be sure you're hydrated. To stay hydrated, stop at every water stop during the race.

- You might feel that the pace is too slow, but resist the temptation to speed up, at least for now. There's an old saying among marathoners that the race begins at twenty miles. If you still feel like you have plenty in the tank at twenty miles, speed up gradually. You'll pass lots of people who went out too fast and "hit the wall." Once that happens, even walking is difficult.

Conclusion

If you follow this training plan closely—and resist the temptation to go out too fast—you should finish your first marathon. You may have to walk a little, and I promise that your body will hurt in ways you never imagined. But when you cross that finish line you'll have accomplished something great—running 26.2 miles.

Good luck and have fun—you're going to want to do this again!

Post-Script—Something Cool for After Your Marathon (Or Before): Remember that 10K you ran at week nine? Take that time and multiply it by five. How close do you get to your actual marathon time? It should be a decent prediction!

See *Nuts and Bolts* for training schedules for the half marathon and marathon at various pace targets.

▼▼▼

4 Friends— and Competitors

▼ ▼ ▼ ▼ ▼ ▼ ▼ ▼

I met Bob Marty at a neighborhood barbecue—the kind of event where everyone in the subdivision is supposed to get know each other and become best buddies. In this case, it actually worked.

My family and I had moved into our new house in August of 1988, and we had been in the neighborhood for about nine months. It was a brand-new community, sanguinely named Saginaw Hills, although it wasn't actually very hilly, and the lone pond was actually man-made. The man who made it, an eccentric, rather hefty developer named John Cooch, owned the largest estate in the neighborhood—not to mention a helicopter, a fact that delighted my sons—and had also seen fit to name the streets after his family, resulting in such tasteful creations as "Tammy Lane."

The barbecue was held at the Cooch residence, a white farmhouse with horses out back, and it didn't take me long to gravitate towards Bob—a friendly, grounded, authentic individual in the midst of all the hubbub.

And, as I quickly learned, a fellow runner.

Bob was bigger than me, taller and more solid—obviously in good shape, but lacking a traditional runner's physique. So I have to admit I was a bit skeptical when he told me his marathon PR.

"Two hours and forty-three minutes," he said, with a small smile on his face.

"Really," I said.

"Really," he answered.

Despite all the lessons I had learned from my first marathon—and the many others I had run since then—I was still trying to break three hours. The closest I had come was 3:02.

I immediately knew exactly what I needed to do. I needed to start running with this guy. In my experience, a good running partner is crucial to developing your potential, to pushing you to be your best. And sometimes just to getting you out the door. Bob and Nelson Williams—who I met not long after and quickly included in our group runs—are the best examples of that in my life. The two of them shaped me as a runner and a person over more than twenty years.

Bob helped me in a number of ways. We would meet at his place and run west, heading down a long country road called Zeeb, and I quickly learned what gave him his edge: hard work and sheer persistence. Whatever he may have lacked in pure talent he made up for in spades through training and discipline. During Vietnam he was a drill sergeant in the army, and I almost pity his recruits. The guy can push himself harder than anyone I've ever met.

I thought I got an early start on the day, but Bob liked to run even earlier. He worked in Detroit for an auto parts supplier and liked to run before work—meaning 5:15 in the morning. Sometimes if he had an early meeting we would need to meet at 4:15 A.M. Let me say that again: 4:15 A.M. It was crazy, but we did it.

Running with Bob, I became a more consistent runner and amassed more miles. It didn't matter what the weather or season was—we ran. Raining? We ran. Snowing? We ran. Temperatures in single digits? We ran. He also held to a high-mileage regimen than I was used to. I had been averaging thirty-five to forty miles a week, but Bob believed in running sixty to seventy. Sometimes even 100. On Sundays we did our long run, anywhere from fifteen to twenty miles. I dreaded them, but I did them, and eventually even enjoyed them. The only thing I refused to do was run on Saturdays—my body needed at least a day to recover. Bob, on the other hand, ran seven days a week. Well, he could have it.

But more important than the numbers was the energy. When we ran the Zeeb Loop—about eight miles total—we were always feeding off each other. We did it in sixty to sixty-six minutes each time. On days when he felt good and my legs were sluggish, he would set the pace and I would try to stay with him. On other days the roles reversed themselves. On the rare day that I really struggled, Bob might run ahead a few yards, but he would always double back to check how I was doing. He was very thoughtful that way.

On days when we both felt energetic we would set a torrid pace right from the start. Our legs felt good and strong, our breathing was smooth, our bodies synchronized as if in a trance. We glided through the air—effortless, even though we were running at a seven-minute pace. I'd pick up the pace and within seconds Bob would be right next to me. Then Bob would start edging ahead, and I would match him step by step.

Neither one of us said a word. We knew we had it. In the last half mile we would give it everything and hit an all-out sprint to the finish. Two predators totally focused on our prey. There was no telling who was going to win, but whoever did deserved it.

"Great run," I'd say.

"I couldn't push it anymore," he'd reply.

We were completely drained, but it felt good. Bob estimated that we'd finish those runs at a six-minute pace. He's not one to exaggerate. I'd go to work feeling pumped, and it would last all day long. I'd tell anyone about it who was willing to listen, and probably a few who weren't. I converted many a patient into runners that way—although some of them probably just thought I was nuts.

And then there were the other kinds of mornings. When Bob and I were both running on empty, and we struggled to keep even a slow pace. On those days we were just happy to get it done. In some ways, those are the times having a running partner counts most—not when you're both at your best, but when you're both at your worst.

Those are the times our other friend, Nelson Williams, really steps up. One of my favorite Nelsonisms is "It's the perceived effort that counts in a run." Think about that—not your finish time, just how hard you try. Pure optimism, pure attitude, and exactly what you need when the chips are down. Not to mention a great sense of humor and an infectious laugh, the perfect comic relief on a hard run. That's why I liked Nelson from the moment I met him in the Summer of 1991.

It was a Sunday in August, and I was just finishing up a ten-mile run near my house when I noticed another runner jogging in my direction. I had never seen him before, so I waved and asked him how far he was going. It may seem a little bizarre to just start a conversation with an absolute stranger, but that's what makes the running community so special—I really do feel like I share a bond with other runners, whether I technically know them or not.

Before I knew it, I had joined Nelson for a few extra miles. He had just moved to Michigan from Iowa for an engineering job. He may have been good at numbers, but he was even better at talking—something that's just as important in a running buddy as being competitive.

By the time we parted ways, we had done five more miles, I was comfortably back home and Nelson was still a good four miles from his house. "You left me to die!" Nelson joked. "And you made me run twice as far as I wanted to!"

I could tell I was going to get along with this guy.

I got his number, called him up, and over the next few weeks we did a few "getting to know each other" runs, like junior high schoolers on their awkward first dates. Even though I could tell he wasn't in the best of shape, I soon invited him to join me and Bob on some of our longer, harder runs.

"I get it," Nelson said in one of his many Nelsonisms. "The easy runs were bait, and now you're going to put the hammer down!"

Although it took Nelson a while to get up to our level, he added some good mischief to our runs. Nelson is tough and strong, but he's also a little guy, with sharp features, deep laugh lines in his face, a sparkle in his eye, and a broad impish grin—kind of like our own personal leprechaun. And competition is even better when it's fun. Or funny.

We had recently switched to a new course, after I came close to badly injuring myself in a five-foot-deep ditch on the side of the Zeeb Loop. Now we were running into the city—far less ditch-prone—down Stadium Boulevard, creating another eight-mile loop. But just like before we loved to push each other to do our best—and it just so happened that Nelson and I did our best on a day Bob was out of town for work.

Nelson and I were seven miles into the course—not even trying for a great time, really—when he looked down at his watch and gasped.

"Oh my God," he said, practically giggling. "You won't believe this."

"Believe what?" I said.

"No, I can't tell you till we finish!"

We finished, and he told me—fifty-eight minutes and thirty-three seconds, a new record for the Stadium Loop by two minutes. Now, seven-minutes a mile may not seem earth-shattering, but when you consider that the track was eight miles and we weren't even racing, it was definitely something to be proud of. Nelson certainly thought so.

"Quick!" he said. "Give me a piece of paper and a marker." Now he really was giggling—gleefully—as the light danced in his blue eyes. I had no idea what he was up to until I saw him post the note on Bob's front door: *58:33—course record—wish you were here!*

He even insisted on us taking a picture with the note and his watch—as proof of our mighty, Bob-less accomplishment.

Nelson and I laughed and laughed. We couldn't wait to see Bob's response. But competitor that he was, Bob wouldn't even give us the satisfaction. He never mentioned the note, wouldn't even acknowledge seeing it, even though the note had "mysteriously" vanished by the time Nelson drove by a short time later. For all Bob's denials, however, something interesting happened a couple months later.

Bob, Nelson and I were doing our usual early-morning run when shortly after we started Nelson and I noticed that Bob was unusually quiet—and running with a lot of determination. A mile from the start he was already fifteen or twenty yards ahead of us, and he was not slowing down. A mile later he was forty yards ahead.

"You know," Nelson said, "I bet he's trying to break our record."

We exchanged a worried look—and took off after him. Soon I had caught up to Bob, with Nelson not far behind. But Bob was on a mission. He never said a word, just breathing hard and running harder. I glanced behind me—Nelson was with us, but losing ground. I stayed focused, matching Bob step for step.

Our feet pounded the blacktop as we rounded the corner into Saginaw Hills. My driveway served as our official finish line—like we were two kids racing for bragging rights after school. We hit the home stretch and I knew it was going to be a classic head-to-head finish with my old friend and competitor. Running in sync, feeding off each other, pushing each other as hard as we could.

We finished completely drained—and in a dead tie. At least that's what I like to think. Our time? 56:18. Carving a whopping two minutes off the previous record. We high-fived it, too out of breath to talk.

Nelson finished a few seconds behind us—a personal record, but still…behind us.

"You were trying to break our record the whole time!" Nelson shouted at Bob, laughing as he tried to catch his breath. "Don't you deny it!"

But deny it is exactly what Bob did.

"I just felt good this morning," he said. "That's all."

The giant grin he wore on his face for days afterwards suggested otherwise.

It's funny—at its most basic level, running is a very individualistic sport. Yet it's also been the source of my greatest, most endearing friendships. Sure, it's great to train with other people. Yes, the competition will help you be a better runner. Absolutely, the company will keep you from getting bored. But it's more than all that. And ironically, the special bond that runners form lies in just how isolating running can be.

Running is, by nature, lonely. There is no ball to pass. It's just you against the road, you against your PR, you against the world. You against yourself. But when you run with other people, with your friends, you transcend that isolation. You are no longer alone, in the truest sense of the word. When Bob and Nelson and I sprinted toward that finish line, when one of us would pick up the pace and the others one would match him, we weren't individuals anymore. We were operating as a single body, a single will, a single being. In those moments, you feel like you're part of something bigger than yourself. It's an almost religious experience. Take it from me—I grew up in a convent.

Bob, Nelson and I never broke the record for the Stadium Loop again. Why would we? After all, it was just a training run.

▼▼▼

▼ NELSON'S CORNER 4 ▼   Teaming Up for Success

When I began running thirty-two years ago I was fortunate to meet a few runners with more training and racing experience than me. Running with them has really helped me improve, and finding great partners can help you too.

Here are some specific training suggestions to help you and your running partner get the most out of your runs.

Drill One: Interval Training or Repeats

Run **quarter-mile repeats** on a track with someone of equal or superior ability to your own. (I have never had a problem finding someone better than me, so no excuses!) Interval training is not easy—especially learning how to pace yourself—and having a partner can be a great way to find your natural rhythm.

Start off with a fifteen-minute warm-up. After that, have your partner time you doing your first quarter. Now switch off with your partner—as you rest, he or she can do their first quarter, and you can time them. Note how you feel with your initial pace, and then run a second lap. If the first lap felt too slow, the second lap should be five seconds faster—have your partner call out your time as you run so you can adjust your speed accordingly.

Continue to alternate running and resting with your partner for a total of four fast quarters. The pace you end up with should feel slightly uncomfortable, but one you can keep up for all four quarters. Until you gain some experience, your partner's feedback will keep you from over extending yourself and burning out. You can also keep track of each other's form, and even start racing each other as you become more fit.

After three weeks of four quarters, increase to six quarters for the next two weeks, then eight for the next two. Don't go beyond eight quarters until you're running at least twenty-five miles a week. Running repeats will significantly improve your time in a 5K or a 10K, and make the race more fun.

Drill Two: Group Runs

The objective here is to run with more intensity than in your usual solo training. The first thing to take care of is finding your group.

If you don't have people you can ask, try your local running store's web site—chances are they sponsor or at least advertise some group runs. Join a group that trains slightly faster than what you're used to. Not only will you pick up speed as you try to keep up with the pack, but you can also discuss other training techniques with your new friends.

Drill Three: Hill Repeats

The major component of this drill is, yes, a hill. (Shocking, right?) Track a quarter mile uphill, then head back down to the base to get started. The goal: three successive hills at a faster time, with no rests in between. Make sure to run them with our partner—both to push you, and to potentially call an ambulance!

Important: Make sure you do a mile jog as a warm-up and a cool-down. Hills, especially steep ones, are rough on your leg muscles.

Drill Four: Chases

This technique really takes advantage of your competitive instinct. It's very similar to the repeats we've already talked about, with one major difference: your partner will start the quarter mile five yards ahead of you (or vice versa). The trailing runner then tries to catch the leader before the finish line.

This is a more advanced workout, so make sure you've done the basic quarter-mile repeats for at least a month before trying it. When you do, alternate chases with the basic repeats every other week—your running mechanics and overall speed will improve. And as you'll soon find out, starting with a five-yard lead isn't necessarily easier than being the chaser.

▼▼▼

Feel free to up the distance of any of the interval workouts—half miles or even full miles. Runners working toward longer races like a ten miler or a half-marathon may prefer longer repeats at a slightly slower pace than the quarters. There are many variations on the drills I've described here—use your imagination as your fitness improves.

Good running!

▼▼▼

In the Spring of 1983, I decided to tackle THE marathon. The biggest, the best, the granddaddy of them all—the Boston Marathon.

Boston is the flagship marathon—not just of this country, but the entire world. The race has an amazing history, starting in 1897 without one missed marathon since then. No other marathon can even come close. But it's more than just the numbers—there's an aura to Boston, a mystique. Whether it's the old engravings of the original races or the modern records set by stars like Bill Rodgers and Johnny Kelley or the eternal challenge of "Heartbreak Hill," Boston is special. As a runner, you haven't arrived until you've run Boston. And as for fans—everyone knows that Boston is 26.2 miles, but tell someone you're running a different marathon and they'll stare in bewilderment. "Really? How long is that one?"

Any marathon other than Boston simply isn't a marathon.

And it was almost completely ruined for me by a couple dollops of spoiled cream in my coffee. As it happened, though, the combination of bad dairy, a sour stomach and a historic race not only led to one of my most memorable marathons, but also to a lesson about pacing—and life—that I'll never forget.

▼▼▼

As one of the world's elite marathons—Boston is one of five World Marathon Majors—it's not enough to sign up for Boston. You need to qualify for Boston.

My qualifying race was one of the strongest, most complete marathons of my life. Not only was it yet another Detroit

Marathon—my third, in October of 1983—but it was also instigated by that original provocateur herself, Diane Navarre, from the sailing club. Somehow getting it into her head that I had to do the Boston, Diane actually called up the Boston Athletic Association to find out the qualifying time for my age group, forty and up.

"You only need a 3:10!" she shouted over the phone.

"Diane, I'm with a patient!" I said. "Can't this wait?" She remained undeterred by the demands of my dental practice.

"You can do it, you can do it!"

It turned out she was right. I clocked a 3:02:14, maintaining a fairly steady pace alongside Mike Carter throughout the run—6:50 over the first ten miles, then hovering around 7:00 for the next ten, and a little over 7:00 for the final six, including a final mile of exactly seven minutes. Diane and her friend even ran the last mile with me—panting even more than I was, I'm proud to say—and cheered as I crossed the line under a crystal blue sky. They weren't the only ones cheering.

"I did it!" I shouted. "I did it!"

It was the mirror opposite of my first marathon, two years prior. This time around, the biggest problem I had was getting to the starting line in Windsor. Let's just say that the Canadian border guard wasn't too pleased when I proudly announced that I had been born in Bethlehem, Palestine (which I was) and promptly followed by asking where to find a good Italian restaurant, because I needed to carbo load (which I did).

So I must admit I was feeling pretty confident going into Boston six months later, in April 1984.

Although I had lost my training partner—Mike had actually moved to Boston for a teaching position—I had managed to keep a steady, strong training schedule by myself. It totaled about forty-five miles a week, and with a certain amount of poetic justice, basically followed the *Free Press* plan I had ignored for my first marathon: shorter mileage on Mondays and Fridays, speed work on Tuesdays, hills on Thursdays, six to ten miles on Wednesdays—and on Sundays, the big daddy, usually fourteen to eighteen miles. Saturdays, as usual, were my day of rest.

And, even though an injury prevented him from ultimately qualifying that year, Mike promised to run the last ten miles with me. Not only that, but now that he lived in Boston I could even stay at his place, virtually giving me a home court advantage.

My brother Francois and I arrived in Boston two days before the Monday afternoon race. Seven years younger than me, with long, wild, curly red hair, Francois wasn't a runner himself, but he loved to explore new cities and I figured that his easily excitable, positive—some would say flamboyant—nature would be a huge bonus for the marathon.

Francois and I stayed with Mike, in his tiny, nearly bare apartment. Sleeping on the hard wood floor was a little painful, especially for someone with my bony frame, but mostly I was focused on checking out the course I had heard so much about. On Saturday we drove to the start in the small town of Hopkinton, southwest of the city, and traveling all the way to the finish on Boylston Street, in the heart of Boston. Even though I now had a fair amount of experience running marathons, I must say this one was daunting. The history of the course was itself awe-inspiring—from the classic Cape Cod houses and the ivy walls (and cute co-eds) of Wellesley College to the gothic halls of Boston College and the famous Citgo Sign outside Fenway Park.

But more than the classic character, there were hills. Oh, there were hills. Up and down, up and down, up and down, they started at the beginning and never let up. For the first time I could see why Heartbreak Hill, in particular, had earned its name. "Hill" is deceptive, as it's actually a series of three hills—so long and far you can't even see the end. More runners drop out there than anywhere else on the course.

"Damn," Francois said. "I can't believe you're going to run all those hills. That doesn't seem like twenty-six miles—it seems like fifty!"

Hmm, I thought. So much for that positivity.

Thankfully, a bad attitude had never been a problem of mine, and it wasn't now. Soon, however, I—and my stomach—would encounter something far more difficult to overcome.

Monday morning was gray, bleak and drizzling—actually an improvement over Sunday, when it poured all day long and well into the night. I put on my burgundy running shorts and a black, long-sleeve turtleneck with a blue wool hat and wool mittens that I usually used for cross country skiing. I was ready for the elements. The rain had woken me up several times, my thin sleeping bag hadn't provided much comfort, and I was looking forward to putting something in my belly before the long run, which started at noon.

As for Francois, he was sound asleep, huddled under a mass of blankets on the floor, with no interest in going anywhere.

Mike and I found a small country restaurant, a mom-and-pop kind of place. I didn't want to overload, so I kept my breakfast down to toast and jelly, and of course my standard cup of coffee. With cream—perhaps a throwback of my days at College des Frères, when I loved to sip *café au lait*. The stuff didn't look very fresh and I should've known better. But I did not, and I drank the entire foul brew down to the very last drop.

It still infuriates me to this day. That damn cream.

Mike dropped me off in Hopkinton at about 10:45. I took shelter by a nearby school, but I was warm in my wool and any rain had died down to a light sprinkle. It was just minutes before the twelve o'clock start when it hit me.

Gurgle. Gurgle gurgle gurgle. Splutter.

We've all been there before, so you know what I'm talking about. My stomach just wasn't right. It was churning, bloated, even making funny noises.

Skrunk gurgle splutter.

Ugh. That damn cream.

I proceeded to the start line, trying to ignore the ominous sensations and still hoping for the best. My plan was to run a sub-three-hour marathon or about a 6:50 pace. After all, I had three marathons under my belt and I had improved my time in each one. In my last marathon I had been only two minutes and fourteen seconds off. I had trained well and hard and I was in the best shape of my life.

The gun went off. Back then the qualifying standards were much tighter and the field was much smaller—probably between 5,000 and 6,000 runners—so I had already managed to position myself to the front. But it wasn't more than a half mile before the pain in my side became too hard to ignore. In moments I completely cramped up and was forced to come to a full stop.

Thankfully, I had brought some toilet paper. I staggered off to the side and ducked behind some bushes to get some relief. It wasn't good enough. I tried to run again, but the cramps were so bad I was having trouble breathing. My body was bent over as I tried to get rid of my gas. One guy even stopped long enough to ask if I was okay—"Just breathe deeply and exhale slowly, you'll feel better"—before taking off. "Come on," I thought. "Feel better? I'm dying here!"

I had pity for the other runners around me; now I knew how Debbie felt.

I kept trying to run, but I kept cramping up. This was Boston, dammit—I had to make it!

The pain, the stopping and the starting, went on for twenty or thirty minutes, but it seemed like an eternity. Finally, miraculously, my body worked the evil dairy demon that was plaguing it out of its system. My body felt depleted, but at least I didn't have a thousand needles piercing my abdomen. I was way behind my pace—no way I could get under three hours now—but I was just happy I could run again.

I picked up the pace. At mile sixteen, I reached the base of Heartbreak Hill. If I thought it looked bad before, it looked much worse now—like a long, winding, never-ending mountain. Suddenly Mike seemed to come out of nowhere—as promised, there to run the last ten miles—like a puppet with spring-loaded legs, jumping up and down, raring to go.

"What happened to you?" he said, his brow creased in concern. "I was worried!"

In a couple clipped sentences I quickly explained my previous ordeal.

"How do you feel now?" he asked.

I looked at my watch. It had been just over two hours since the start of the marathon. To reach my goal of three hours I'd have to cover ten miles in less than sixty minutes. It seemed impossible, especially considering the state I was in.

"I can make it," I said.

He didn't hesitate.

"Well, then," he said. "Let's go."

We took off. What happened then was nothing short of a Boston marathon miracle. Or at the time, at least that's what I thought.

We zigged and zagged past one runner after another, bobbing and weaving like there was no tomorrow, to hell with the hills. We must've been doing six minutes a mile. I'd never had this much energy at the end of a race, much less one that was twenty-six miles long.

The last three to four miles were a dead sprint. Mike was usually faster than me, but not on this day—I was right by his side. The crowds must've been at least ten deep, cheering louder and louder the closer we got to the finish line. I rocketed through the last few yards like there was no tomorrow, and when I crossed people were screaming as if I had won the race. Some runners, I'm sure, wondering if I had actually run the entire thing.

It was phenomenal. It was Boston.

After that agonizing start, I ended up finishing feeling better and stronger than I ever had—or ever would—again. And my time? Three hours and seven minutes. Short of my sub-three-hour goal, and five minutes slower than my qualifying run—but considering how I started, I was amazed.

Maybe the spoiled cream was actually some kind of super fuel?

That clearly wasn't the answer. But in a sense it wasn't far off—even though I didn't really understand the implications until many years later. My first Boston was the exact inverse of my first marathon. As sick as it made me, the bad dairy had also forced me to go out incredibly slow, saving everything I had for the last ten miles—when I really opened up and blew everyone away.

What I've realized is that finishing strong is just as important—maybe more so—than starting fast. In racing and in life. All of these stories from my youth are fun—at least I hope they are—but what would they mean if I weren't still running today, at the age of sixty-eight? Memories can only do so much, can only last so long. Ultimately, the challenge of life is to learn how to keep growing, to keep getting better, to not peak too soon. Not in a way that's measured by times or records or statistics, but by how you feel about the things that really matter—family, friends, spirituality and life. That's what I mean when I say it's good to go out on top.

I have run the Boston Marathon seventeen times over the past twenty-eight years. To this day, my first Boston is my fastest Boston. I've never broken three hours in a marathon, and at my age probably never will. Who knows? Maybe if I had listened more carefully to the sounds of my gurgling stomach, that would be different

I can tell you one thing, though—marathon or no, I avoid cream at all costs. And I always take my coffee black.

▼▼▼

▼ NELSON'S CORNER 5 ▼   Learning to Pace Yourself

Teaching yourself to run at an even pace in a long race is a challenge for the distance runner. But to run your best, you must learn pacing.

The key to maintaining consistent pace is constantly making small corrections in speed to accommodate your fitness level, the course's temperature, wind, hills, running surface, distance, and many other variables. That's a lot to manage, so it's best to start out small and work your way up. The key to this, as in so much of running, is repetition.

That's right, we're doing **more interval training**! (I can hear the groan from the crowd already.)

Come on—intervals are fun! You'll need a watch with a lap timer, a track for distance accuracy, and about an hour a week for six to eight weeks.

Quarter Intervals

Start out as always by warming up with at least a mile jog, then a two-minute rest.

For your first quarter-mile, run at a faster pace than usual. At the halfway mark (i.e., after an eighth of a mile), mark your time on your watch. (Most runner's watches have an easy function that allows you to record these "splits.") Make sure to get your time at the end of the quarter too. Compare your first half-quarter with your second half—the splits should be close to the same.

Rest two minutes, then try again. As you run, listen to your body. Work on getting the two half-quarters to match both in time and in the effort you put in. Paying attention to how you feel will help you develop your "internal clock."

Do this drill until you can run **four quarters in a row** (plus two minute breaks), with the first and second halves of each within three seconds of each other.

Once you've mastered this—be patient, it will take several weeks—move on to...

Half Intervals

This is the exact same as the quarter-mile intervals except—you guessed it—now you'll be doing half-miles, and checking your split after each quarter-mile. Once you can do three halves in a row—with the quarter-mile splits each within three seconds of each other—move on to...

Mile Intervals

Note: This drill is for more advanced runners. If you run less than twenty-five miles a week, stick to quarters and halves.

For mile intervals, check your time after each quarter-mile split. Your four laps should be within five seconds of each other. Practice this drill until you can complete three one-mile repeats—with a five-minute break, or a quarter-mile walk, between each. Once you get to the point where each of your miles is within ten seconds of the others, you'll have a much better feeling for your limits and how to run within them.

The Next Level

Want a really cool challenge? Try recording your splits and interval times blind—in other words, don't look at your watch while you're running them. Better yet, have a partner do it for you. Then compare your times when you've finished. If your times are almost identical, congratulations—you're a master of pacing your runs.

The Highest Level

Move from the track to the road. There you'll have to not only listen to your body, but also gauge differences in weather condition and terrain—essentials for any long-distance runner. You can also increase your intervals to as long as three or four miles, or just compare your mile splits on a standard four-mile run.

Don't get discouraged—it will take even longer to find an even pace out on the road. After all, that wind, those hills, that party last night…

Conclusion

These drills will teach you to compare your pace with how your body feels—how to calibrate and balance the two. Once you have internalized these "speed limits," you can adjust your pace during a training run or a race to stay in your zone. Do these drills regularly and your sense of pace will steadily improve along with your fitness!

▼▼▼

6 Blazing Trails

▼ ▼ ▼ ▼ ▼ ▼ ▼

Every inch of the earth was buried in pure, white snow, over seven inches of it newly fallen. Every tree, every bush, every branch, every twig. And I was in the middle of it all. Stuck. At least for the time being.

"Hey Dave," I called to my running buddy, David Bach. "I think I'm a little—"

I finished the sentence with a grunt as I wrenched my ankle free from the icy bramble. I was crawling under a giant fallen tree, my body covered in snow, trying to work my way through the narrow trail—or what was left of it. Sound a bit perilous? It was. But that was the point.

That was the Potawatomi Trail.

Dave had no problem waiting for me as I finally burrowed my way out, staggering to my feet. It was February 2006, I had run the Houston Marathon just three weeks earlier, my legs were tiring, and I didn't want to aggravate my chronically injured hamstring. But in weather like this we weren't setting any speed records on our thirteen-mile course, so we decided to walk for a few minutes.

It was worth it. The phrase "winter wonderland" is used a lot, but nothing better describes what surrounded us. The Potawatomi is located in the Pinckney Recreation Area, by the banks of Silver Lake, about a thirty-minute drive from Ann Arbor. It's nature at its purest—and harshest. Treacherous hills, narrow dirt trails, twisted trees, ragged roots and rocks of all sizes. And this morning it was all white, and all spectacular.

The snow was so thick it weighed down tree branches, forcing them to droop low and touch the ground. This time we had managed to squeeze underneath, but sometimes we had to detour off-trail. In some spots we were lucky if we could even see the trail. The fact that we were the only human beings for miles just added to the surrealness of the situation. No traffic, no civilization, no nothing. The only thing we could hear were the sporadic cries of the few birds that stuck around for winter.

Dave and I were both well-equipped for our adventure. Me in my running tights, waterproof top and trusty purple Jackson Hole ski hat, which has practically been through more races than I have at this point. And Dave—a stylish runner, even for a spry, accomplished cardiologist—in a bright blue jacket and black ski hat, his round, silver-rimmed glasses barely peaking out under his hat. Of course, colors barely mattered at this point—whatever we had on was caked in snow.

After my hamstring loosened up, we started jogging again, shaking off the snow and cold. It was slow going, tedious. But it was also serene. We never even thought about cutting the run short.

▼▼▼

I first heard about the Potawatomi in 1990, from Randy Step, who owns Running Fit, an amazing store that carries just about anything a runner would ever need. Randy had founded a race called Dances with Dirt—which proudly bears the slogan "Not For Wimps." The T-shirts even feature a disclaimer stating that the organizers aren't responsible for any bodily harm or death that results from the run.

This, I thought, is the race for me.

That said, even I wasn't up for the ultimate challenge—the full marathon. Like most sane human beings, I opted for the

Dance's half-marathon option. Only ten percent of the entire field—which itself only number 250—went for the full twenty-six miles, and I could tell why. People spoke of the trail with awe, admiration, even fear. And these weren't newbies, these were seasoned runners in the Ann Arbor Track Club.

With all the natural obstacles—rocks, roots, holes, sawed-off tree stumps—Potawatomi wasn't just a test of cardio but of strength, agility and endurance, in the fullest sense of the word. That wasn't even taking into account the weather. A little bit of rain and you'd find yourself in buckets of mud, slipping and sliding all over the dangerously steep hills. And I had no off-road experience. I was a city-boy, born and bred. I heard all the talk, but I had no idea what to expect.

The morning of the race I brought a map, some bandages, extra clothes, a second pair of shoes, and even food and water. Hell, I thought, what if I got lost in the wilderness? Who knew how long it would take for someone to find me? I wasn't screwing around—I was preparing for battle. So was my competition.

When I got to Silver Lake at 7 A.M.—over an hour before the start—a hundred guys were already there, getting ready. These weren't your ordinary runners. They looked lean and mean, ready to do battle. Was this an amateur running race or the sequel to "Mad Max Beyond Thunderdome?"

I needed to get a grip.

I joined the crowd and positioned myself in the middle of the pack. The full-marathon runners had started at 8 A.M., a half-hour before us. The trail was so narrow at points that we had a staggered start, with groups of us taking off ten minutes apart. I was part of the first wave, but I kept a slower pace—because I wanted time to adjust, and because I had just run the Boston Marathon six days earlier. (Yes, I'm a glutton for punishment.)

But after two or three miles I started to get into a rhythm. My legs loosened up, and instead of walking gingerly around the roots, stones and stumps, I attacked them—dipping, dodging, jumping over everything in my way. Not only was I not afraid anymore, I was having a blast. My small frame, light weight and strong ankles gave me a huge advantage in the tough terrain over bigger, more awkward runners.

I passed people left and right, even in the narrowest parts of the trail.

"Nice footwork!" someone called as I rushed by.

A man in front of me tripped over a small stump, tumbling down a steep embankment.

"Hey, are you alright?" I called.

He just muttered and shook his head, more embarrassed about tripping than anything else, so I forged ahead. The sounds of the birds and critters, the fresh smell of nature gave me an energy I didn't know I had. The rapidly changing trail forced me to stay hyper alert and aware, making me run even harder.

I passed easily fifty to sixty runners in the second half of the race, finishing in a time of an hour and thirty eighth minutes and winning my age group handily. Whereas many of the other runners were marred by bumps and bruises and even some blood, I came out completely unscathed.

"It's unfair!" Nelson told me later. "You're like the Last of the Mohicans. You draw strength from the dirt!"

So began my love affair with running in the wilderness. But it wasn't always that painless. If it had been I think it would've held far less appeal.

My next run in the Potawatomi saw the realization of my initial worst fear, when Bob Marty and I got completely lost in the woods. We had a map, of course, which Bob had tucked under his lucky Ronzoni Pasta cap, from a big pasta dinner we had eaten before Boston. But that day the cap wasn't quite lucky enough—not only was it raining, a slow, steady drizzle, but the trees were all waterlogged, and Bob and I had to slither through soaking wet branches just to make it through the trail.

By the time we were six miles into the run, the map had turned into a soggy blob of unusable mush—and we found ourselves at a split in the trail. Left or right? When in doubt I always go right, so right it was. We were completely wrong. But we found our way back to the finish, clocked about two hours, and have stayed with the "wrong" trail ever since—so we could improve our time.

On another run, despite the advantage of my sure feet and Nelson's so-called "dirt effect," I took a tumble over a tiny tree stump, just barely getting my gloved-hands in front of me as I flew face-first toward the trail. My body was battered and my left shoulder banged up—but that adventure was minor compared to another summer when my main motivation to finish wasn't to beat my time but escape the clouds of mosquitoes and deer flies relentlessly swarming me, David Bach and our friend Steve Bolling.

I know, it sounds like something out of an old Bugs Bunny Looney Toons cartoon—until you actually experience it. The air was so thick with bugs it was hard to see, like some biblical plague. I had to keep my mouth shut so I wouldn't swallow any. Dozens of deer flies attacked Dave's back and neck, biting him at will. Incredibly aggressive, sticking with us no matter how fast we went. We even tried stripping branches off trees to use as switches as we ran, swatting them off in vain. If we hadn't made it out of there, I'm convinced they literally would've devoured us, leaving nothing the next day but a group of immaculately cleaned skeletons. When we did finally escape we felt an amazing sense of accomplishment—not only did we run a hard thirteen miles, but we also survived.

Off-road running really can be dangerous, and it isn't for everyone. As accomplished of an athlete as he is, Nelson loathes running the Potawatomi—perhaps part of the reason he's so admiring of my own abilities. He worries about injuries and thinks his ankles are better suited for flat, even roads, and I had to pester him for weeks to get him to try it.

When Nelson finally did run the Potawatomi, he really struggled over the last four miles. Bob and I stayed with him, goading him on, telling him not to give up—on steep hills, Bob would even physically push him from behind, pinching his ass jokingly to get him to move faster.

In the last half-mile, Bob and I surged ahead. From the finish we could see Nelson in the distance, hunched over, his head dangling as he struggled to shuffle his feet. His face was flushed, sweat streaming down his forehead and cheeks, his glasses fogged up and covered with dirt. I walked towards him, and he finally managed to raise his head. I extended my right hand. "Nelson," I said, "welcome to the Potawatomi Trail."

Nelson told me later that if he had possessed any strength at all in his body, he would have killed me. You know, I think he actually would have.

What's worse, I probably deserved it.

▼▼▼

Hitting the trails and going off-road can be great training for a runner. Not only does it challenge you physically—strengthening your ankles, improving your agility and building muscle on all the hills—but it keeps you sharp and fresh mentally too. Running roads can be hypnotic with their long, steady rhythm. But the wilderness keeps you—quite literally—on your toes, constantly engaged with your environment, struggling to surmount the latest obstacle in your path.

But running the Potawatomi is about more for me than the physical and the mental. There's something deeply spiritual about being in nature, surrounded by the elements, and having to blaze your own path. Maybe it's because so much of life is also about blazing your own path, on a figurative level. Making your own decisions, choosing the direction that feels right in your gut, having no idea where you're going or where you'll end up—and then just going for it, to hell with the consequences.

Or maybe it's just the sound of a sand hill crane echoing through the hills. The glimmer of sunlight on the stillness of Crystal Lake. And yes, even the buzz of a cloud of angry deer flies.

Whatever it is, with all its hurdles, its fallen trees and narrow, twisted trails, the Potawatomi is one of the few places in the world where I find peace.

▼▼▼

Dave Bach and I finally finished our wintry, snow-capped run in record time—record slow, that is. It took us two hours and forty-five minutes to pound our way through the frozen wilderness.

When we got to the parking lot we whooped and cheered like kids. We even threw a few snowballs. Not so much because we finished, but more because we were overcome by the beauty around us. Everything white, the snow still fresh and unsullied, the forest vast and still like the day of creation. It made us feel young, like we still had our entire lives ahead of us, all the promise, all the possibility, all the joy.

In the end, it felt good to stop.

▼ Nelson's Corner 6 ▼   Wilderness Training

Running on a wilderness trail is unlike running on a paved road—and in many ways, it's superior. The cushioned surface is easier on the body. Woods can be cooler in summer, and shield you from harsh winds in the winter. Adapting to uneven surfaces improves your balance and agility. Roots and holes force you to concentrate and be more alert. Best of all, there is no traffic.

First, though, you need to find a good trail! It should be four to ten miles in length. Contact your local parks and recreation department for some suggestions. Ask at your local running shoe store.

Once you've found a suitable trail, have your running partner join you to try it out. (Make sure you have a map!) Since most trails contain an assortment of hidden obstacles—quick drops, slippery spots, rocks and roots—walk it that first time. Make mental notes as you go. When you do run the course, break it up into smaller pieces at first. Get to know its unique features a little at a time. (Think I'm being overly cautious? Tell that to my joints after years of running the Potawatomi!) Try the following trail exercises:

Exercise 1: Hills

Find a hilly stretch on your trail. Jog slowly through the hills running for five minutes. Marking your finish spot, then return to your starting point. Try this three times with a just two-minute rest between each one. The challenge? See how much farther you can make it each time.

Exercise 2: Twists and Turns

I'll admit it—this one is pretty much the same as Exercise 1, except with lots of corners and sharp turns. Find a winding portion of the trail—something that'll make you zigzag and shift your direction repeatedly. Jog that section, making mental notes of the footing. Go out five minutes, mark the turnaround point, then return to the start. Repeat three times, again trying to cover more of the trail in the same five-minute time limit. Are you good enough to do all the twists and turns at a near sprint? And survive?

Exercise 3

Start at the beginning of the trail. Jog five minutes then walk two minutes. Repeat this process until you have run and walked three times. Then reverse directions and repeat the same process. See if you get back to your starting point before the last two-minute rest has timed out. Now that is a challenge!

These exercises are a fun way to become familiar with your trail. Once you know its characteristics, you will find that running there will make you a stronger runner, and make you feel good at the same time!

▼▼▼

The Farah Family:
Gisele, Nelly, Dad,
Alice, John, Mom,
in front of the "Y"
Jerusalem, 1949

Nazareth, 1956
Boy Scouts

John, far right;
Paul Feher, third
from right;
Eddie our troop leader,
fifth from right

Hebrew teacher, Pnina, John, 1959

Frère Jean, John, 1961

From left: John, Frère Jean; John's classmate Ramsay second from right; far right: Frère Benoit, 1962

Farah family, 1976. Back row: Dad, Emile, Mom, Gisele; front row: John, Alice, Francois, Nelly

John with Chris and Mike, 1979. Gainesville, FL

Chris, Dad, John, Mom, Mike
Flint, MI, 1979

1980, Bob Marty qualifying for the Boston
at the Glass City Marathon
2:49:50

Diane Navarre and Mike Farah
U. of M. Sailing Club, 1982

1983, First Boston,
cold and rainy
3:07

1986, Crim race in a downpour
10 miles, 6:04 pace

1987, Detroit Marathon
3:12

1989, Dexter-Ann Arbor Run,
Half Marathon
6.25 min/mi.

1997, Columbus Marathon
3:04

1994, Nelson and John, Dexter-Ann Arbor Run
Half-Marathon

1997, Burns Park 10K
40:27

Nelson stretching even while on a
camping trip, 1998

1998 Boston Marathon, with Dr. Minoru
Horiuchi, a Board of Governors official

Setting up the finish line
Boston Marathon, 1998

1998, at the finish of the Austin Marathon
3:04

John and Dave at the half-way mark
of a very hot 1999 Boston Marathon, 3:28

2000, London Marathon,
post hamstring injury, 3:33

1999, John and Dave, Detroit Marathon
3:15

2001, Columbus Marathon
3:14 finish

2001, Dances with Dirt,
100 km relay race;
left to right: Dave, Brad,
Sharlene, John, Steve

Bob Marty, John;
pre-race, 2001 Paris Marathon

2001,
Paris Marathon finish
3:23

2004, Nelson and John;
pre-start of Grandma's
Marathon, Duluth, MN

2006, Duluth, MN;
Grandma's Marathon,
walking 21 miles to finish

On the Inca Trail, Machu Picchu, 2006

John in San Francisco? No, Potawatomi,
courtesy of Dave Bach, 2006

Jackie and John in Aspen, 2006

Mike and Chris with John after his
100th marathon, Boston, 2008

Collage of race T-shirts.

others short and stubby, and a few were overweight. But they were doing the best they could do on that day. I gained a new level of respect. Running a three-hour marathon isn't easy—but it may be even harder to run a seven-hour one.

I started talking to some of my fellow marathoners. For many it was their first, and they weren't well-prepared for it. For Tom, a guy in his fifties from Minneapolis, it was his third—and, he told me in no uncertain terms, definitely his last. I walked with him for a mile, but he couldn't even keep up with my slow pace. Debra and Lori, two friends from Chicago, were running as a duo—jogging a bit, then walking. They were in good spirits but I could tell that Lori was having some problems.

Usually I would've been the one to encourage her, but in this case—noticing my injury—they wished me well and moved on.

Reaching the half-way mark, I was still hovering around a sixteen-minute pace when I met Michelle, in her early forties. She was wearing a Great Lakes T-shirt, which made me think of Michigan, but it turned out the shirt was from a 5K race out west, and she was from Los Angeles. This was her first marathon, but she was running really strong, and I thought for sure I wouldn't see her again as she passed me by.

Soon after, I encountered my other new friends, Debra and Lori, again. This time in a much sorrier state. Lori was standing on the side of the road, blood streaming down her bare legs. I came to a dead stop.

"Are you okay?" I asked.

"She'll be fine," Debra said, hovering next to her. "It's just her period."

That was pretty much all I needed to hear.

"Well, good luck!"

I took off as fast as my injury would let me. A few miles later I saw them again. They feeling much better, but Lori still struggling—her legs clean, but one of her shoes tinted red from the blood. I settled for giving them a wave.

Finally I hit mile twenty. I was down to almost fifteen minutes a mile. I was feeling a little better, and I could hear my competitive nature whispering to me, goading me on, pushing me to bite off more than I could chew: "Come on, John! If you run, maybe you can finish under six hours! That would be respectable! Forget about the pain, forget about the injury—just make yourself do it!"

And twenty years earlier, maybe I would've listened. But thankfully I had grown. I couldn't run and I knew it. Why beat myself up over it? I could admit my vulnerability and still be confident. I had been walking for five hours—what was another ninety minutes? Suck it up, stay smart, and don't force it. At least I would finish. That's what mattered.

Two miles later, I saw the one person I had been certain I wouldn't see again—Michelle, the runner from Los Angeles. She had looked really strong before, but she didn't look strong anymore. In fact, she was walking so slow that even I could've passed her.

"Hi, Michelle," I said.

She looked up, smiled, grateful for someone to talk to. I told her to stay with me.

"You can make it," I said. "Just stay focused."

At first she had difficulty keeping pace, but the farther she went, the better she felt. With less than three miles to go, she saw her family on the sidelines, cheering—her husband and two daughters, one of whom had flown out from Boston for the race. Michelle rushed over and they all shared a big group hug. In the last two miles I edged ahead of Michelle, but I knew she would finish just fine.

One person who looked far worse was Lori, of the red-tinted shoes. I saw her again at mile twenty-five—so close to the end—and this time completely alone. Debra had pushed ahead to finish before her. There comes a time in a race when no amount of encouragement is going to help, the body is spent, the legs are gone, every muscle aches and you're simply better off being left alone. At that point, it's a matter of mind over body. I had been there before, and Lori was there now. I didn't see her again.

At long last, after six hours, fourteen minutes and fourteen seconds, I finally crossed the line. It was a sweet finish. In some ways, the sweetest.

The skies had turned a dark, stormy gray, and within minutes it was raining. The holding area was a crush of people, paramedics rushing in to administer CPR to a runner who had just collapsed. Now that's a marathon, ▆▆▆▆▆▆▆.

Nelson found me twenty minutes later. He had waited around for a while after he had finished earlier, convinced I must be right behind him, then decided to go back to the hotel for a quick shower. When he came back he went immediately to the first aid tent to ask if they had treated anyone by my name. The records turned up empty. He started to panic—until he noticed me standing in line at a hot dog stand.

After six hours of walking, I was starving—and craving junk food.

"What happened?" he shouted.

After I told him, Nelson just shook his head in disbelief.

"John," he said, "you are one of a kind."

As I've said before, Nelson has a penchant for overstatement. In reality, it had taken a long time for me to get to this point in my life. Years, actually—and several injuries. And this certainly wouldn't be my last. Just a couple years after Grandma's, in 2009, I injured a whole new body part—my knees, on the incredibly steep downward slopes of the Big Sur Marathon. I'd go back to Jeff Barnett, I'd heal, and who knows—maybe someday I'd get injured again.

But that really didn't matter. I'd learned that to get beyond injury wasn't really about the physical at all. It was about the mental—learning to come to terms with our natural frailty as human beings, our imperfect bodies and imperfectible lives. I would get old, and then older. I'd turn sixty-four, then sixty-five, sixty-six, and hopefully onward. I would get weak, I would get hurt—but there was nothing wrong with that. It was just an opportunity to experience a whole new phase of my life. A completely different type of adventure—like talking to so many amazing people I normally would have never even met during Grandma's Marathon. That hard-earned attitude was how, ultimately, I was able to go not just beyond the pain—but beyond recovery as well.

I was fortunate enough to receive many great compliments after Grandma's, from friends, family, co-workers—all of them saying how impressed they were that I had been able to overcome such a debilitating obstacle.

But the best compliment of all came in an email I received through the *Dental Advisor*, a dental materials journal I publish. The email said: "I am trying to get in touch with John Farah, he ran the last few miles of Grandma's Marathon with me this year and I would very much like to thank him for his support. If you would please forward this message to him and ask him to contact me." It was signed Michelle Schwartz—the first-time marathoner from Los Angeles. She had finished all right, and afterwards she tracked me down on the internet. Michelle and I stay in touch to this day. We still like to share running stories.

▼▼▼

▼ Nelson's Corner 7 ▼ Stretching Program

The following are stretches that I have found very useful in keeping my body more limber, help avoid injuries and recover from injuries when they occur.

NOTE: In most cases, unless indicated otherwise:

- Hold a stretch ten to twenty seconds.
- Do the right and left sides.
- Do three repeats for each side.

1. Hamstring Stretch

Place your foot on a chair or block with your knee straight. Slowly lean forward at the hip keeping your back straight. Keep this position until you feel a stretch in the back of your thigh. Hold for twenty seconds. Do the other leg.

Repeat three times for each leg.

Another way is to place your foot on a kitchen counter—this one is more intense. Lean forward with a straight back as before and hold for twenty seconds. Now do the other leg.

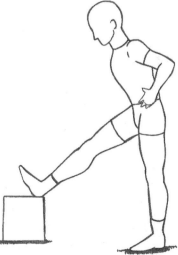

Repeat three times for each leg.

2. Calf and Hamstring Stretch

Stand on a step and hold onto a railing. Place the ball of one foot on the edge of a step, the other foot supporting your weight. Slowly let the heel of your foot drop downward until you feel your calf stretch. Hold for twenty seconds. Do the other leg.

Repeat three times for each leg.

3. Hamstring Stretch, Yoga Style

Stand with your feet approximately eighteen inches apart, with your front foot pointing straight ahead, your back foot at a forty-five-degree angle. Cross your arms behind your back, just above your waist. Lean forward at the hips, keeping your hips parallel to the front wall and your back straight. Feel a stretch in your right hamstring and hip. Hold for thirty seconds.

Turn around, face the wall behind you and repeat the previous stance switching your leg positions. Hold for thirty seconds. Feel a stretch in your left hamstring and hip.

4. Hip Flexor Stretch

Place one knee on the ground and the opposite leg extended forward with your knee bent at ninety degrees. Place your hands on your hips and move your pelvis forward a couple of inches. Feel a stretch in the kneeling leg's groin area (psoas muscle). Hold for twenty seconds. Release, then repeat two more times. Now do the other side.

5. Quadricep Stretch

Stand and hold onto a wall or counter top. Grasp your ankle/foot as shown and pull towards your buttock. Feel the stretch in your quadricep. Hold for twenty seconds. Do the other leg.

Repeat three times.

6. Hip/Knee Stretching/Strengthening

Lie on the floor on your back with your legs outstretched. With one knee bent for stability, raise the other leg about one foot off the floor, keeping your toes pointing toward the ceiling.

Slowly lower your leg to the floor. Repeat twenty times, and then do the other leg.

Repeat this exercise three times.

7a. Hip Adductors Strengthening

Place a ten-inch ball between your legs and squeeze your knees together. Hold for ten seconds.

Repeat twenty times.

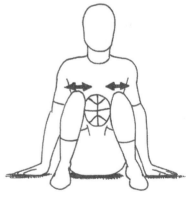

7b. Hip Abductors Strengthening

Place rubber tubing (PowerSystems. com) around both knees and then pull your knees apart. Hold for ten seconds and then bring them back together.

Repeat twenty times.

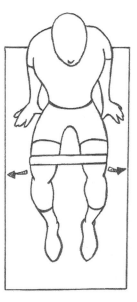

8. Hip Flexor—Warrior Pose

Place your right leg in front with your foot pointing straight ahead and your knee bent at ninety degrees. Your other leg should be straight back behind you with your foot at forty-five degrees. Your trunk should be upright with your hands and arms straight over your head. (This pose is familiar to those who do yoga.)

Tuck and move your pelvis slightly forward and hold for thirty seconds.

Turn around and repeat the pose on the other side.

Repeat the exercise three times.

9. Hip Flexion Resistance

Use circular rubber tubing, about 0.5 inches in diameter (such as the Versa-O, from PowerSystems.com). Step both legs inside the circle. With one leg serving as an anchor, move the other leg forward eight to twelve inches, keeping your knee straight. Repeat ten times.

Repeat the exercise with your other leg.

10a. Lower-Back Strengthening

Lie on your stomach. Raise your right arm and your left leg simultaneously. Hold for two seconds and then repeat with your left arm and your right leg.

Repeat ten times.

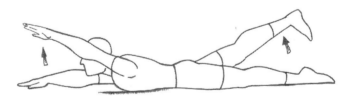

10b. Lower-Back Strengthening

Another variation is to raise both arms and legs and hold for two seconds. Lower arms and legs, and then repeat ten times.

▼▼▼

8 Light On My Feet

▼ ▼ ▼ ▼ ▼ ▼ ▼ ▼

A beautiful, balmy Football Saturday in Ann Arbor, the city buzzing with more than 100,000 fans eager to watch their Wolverines destroy the competition. Except for me. I wasn't sitting on my butt watching football, I was running.

And I had my own competition to focus on.

I was six miles into my run when I saw him. He was a quarter-mile ahead of me on the dusty country road. He was thin and young, with good form and a strong, confident pace. My competitive nature took over immediately. I started closing in, slowly narrowing the gap. My legs felt strong, my mind was clear, my body moving effortlessly, stride after stride. It was a game to me, a game I wanted to win.

I closed to within 200 yards... 160 yards... 135... 100...

So close!

That was when I saw the goat. It, too, was thin and young, with good form and a strong confident pace.

"Baaaaa!"

It darted out of a farm yard, across the street ahead of me and after the other runner. It was as big as a mid-sized poodle—and now it was beating me, dammit!

I started laughing hysterically—who the hell was going to believe this? Even better, the goat was now closing in on my erstwhile competitor, who finally heard the clacking of the tiny hooves behind him. He glanced briefly, kept running—then came to a full stop, absolutely baffled. He looked at me accusingly and said, deadly serious:

"Is this your goat?"

"No," I said, just as seriously. "I thought it was yours."

Somehow, he didn't catch the joke—although I'm sure the goat found it hilarious. The runner muttered something incoherent under his breath, turned and kept running. By that time the goat had also stopped running, looking tired and a bit disoriented. Haven't I said how important the proper training is before a race?

I grabbed my little running buddy by its tiny horns and hoisted him up—it couldn't have weighed more than fifteen pounds and didn't put up much of a struggle. I carried it down the road back to the farm. It had apparently managed to squeeze out of a hole in a fence. The mama goat was bleating frantically, calling for its kid—and its human owner was out in the front yard, searching as well.

"Thank you so much," she said. "Do you want some water?"

I thanked her and kept running. Although I probably should've found out if she had a trainer. That goat showed real potential.

▼▼▼

We can all learn a lot from that goat.

Okay, fine, I'm joking—kind of. I've spoken a lot about the importance of pushing yourself, of never being satisfied with mediocrity, never giving up. But one of the greatest things about running are the simple, silly little stories you accumulate over time. Running is a great way to learn how to relax, have fun, and not take life too seriously. In other words, how to be light on your feet—literally and figuratively.

Not only is that an important thing to do just to feel good and be happy, but it's also important for success. Do I dominate every race I run? Absolutely not. Do I even always achieve the personal goals I set for myself, reaching my optimal time, placement, or improvement? Nope. But I never let that bog me down. Instead, I keep each race in perspective. Sure, I enjoy the victories, but I'm not obsessed with winning, and I never focus on a loss. Most important, I laugh. A lot.

Everyone wants to be the hero. But sometimes it's even more fun to be the goat.

▼▼▼

The 1998 San Francisco Marathon was another race that started with very grand aspirations and ended a little closer to the gutter. Or in this case, the side of a wall.

I was fifty-five years old and I had been running well, clocking two marathons at 3:04 apiece. I was running so well, in fact, that I thought this might be one of the few times I could outrace my friend and trainer, Jeff Barnett. As you know, Jeff is a fantastic runner and an incredible athlete—and he's younger than me—so I knew I'd have to run flawlessly to beat him.

Unfortunately, my bladder did not get the memo.

Halfway into the marathon, all the fluids I had been drinking started to get to me. I was running at an even pace with a guy named David, who I had met along the course, when I promptly announced I needed to find a Porta-John.

"I need to find a Porta-John."

"I know," he said. "You just said that."

We kept an eye out for the next few minutes, but predictably—given my state of dire need—we couldn't find anything.

Anything except for a grubby warehouse surrounded by an old chain link fence and a few neglected shrubs. Perfect!

I ducked around back and started whizzing against the wall as Dave waited around the corner.

"Hey! What do you think you're doing!?!"

The booming voice did not come from Dave. It came from a cop. The question, I assume, was a rhetorical one. And in all honesty, I was so busy relieving myself I didn't even turn to face him. Had I done that, I probably would've gotten in even worse trouble—for obvious reasons.

"Hey! Stop right now!"

I decided not to comply. Again, for obvious reasons.

The officer was a rather rotund fellow, standing next to the wide-open door of his cruiser, which had cornered me—otherwise, maybe I would've taken off and given it a go, seeing as how I was probably a bit quicker on my feet. Instead I waited as the officer issued me a citation. I decided (silently) to nickname him Roscoe, because he reminded me of the inept deputy Roscoe P. Coltrane from my sons' favorite old show, "The Dukes of Hazzard." If you haven't seen the show, it isn't a flattering comparison. He was big, fat, and slow at everything except writing me tickets.

He said the word "citation" in a long, slow drawl— "syyy-tayy-shun"—letting it drip off his big crusty lips. And not only did he take forever just to find the ticket book, which was lost somewhere in the jumbled mess of his front seat, but he even wrote as slowly as humanly possible. As Roscoe filled out the paperwork—for some reason I gave him my real name and address, when I could have easily thrown him off the trail—he lectured me on the inappropriateness of my behavior, my flagrant disregard of private property, and the sacred anti-urinating nature of the social contract to which every single American is a party.

For my part, I just wanted to get back to running.

Roscoe finally released me, and I rounded the corner—only to find Dave still there, waiting. He had used his extra time to urinate himself—right behind Roscoe's car. David was very proud of that. I was proud of him too.

I ended up finishing the race in three hours and twenty-three minutes—ten minutes off schedule. Not surprisingly, I did not beat Jeff Barnett that day.

The cost of the ticket itself was $135, which I had no intention of paying. First I tried an official from the marathon, who sympathetically told me that San Francisco cops were notorious sticklers for such minor foibles as public urination. So I took my case straight to The Man himself, writing a letter to the traffic fines bureau in which I proudly declared: "Obviously, I am not in the habit of relieving myself on a public street." Sure, it was a lie, but I could only hope they wouldn't access my extensive criminal urination record in Ann Arbor.

Thankfully, my wish came true. Two months later, I received an official response:

In re: citation no: CO85234796

Please be advised that this matter was reviewed by Commissioner C. Lyons. You were found guilty of violation PC374.3A and the fine was suspended, therefore, no payment is due. This matter is now closed and no further proceeding is necessary. Thank you.

Who knows? Maybe Commissioner Lyons was a marathon runner too. Or maybe his bladder is even smaller than mine.

▼ NELSON'S CORNER 8 ▼   Running a Faster Marathon

Aha! I bet you thought this would be an easy Nelson's Corner, filled with a bunch of easy runs and jokes, right? Wrong the joke's on you. This is actually one of the harder regimens, for those of you who are already respectable marathon runners but really want to improve your time and your pace.

If you really want to, I guess you can bring a goat along. I guess.

To start off with, you need a very solid base—these drills are not for inexperienced runners. Once you have that foundation, you'll need at least four to six months to prepare for the full marathon. During that time, here's your basic schedule:

Monday	Tuesday	Wednesday	Thursday	Friday	Saturday	Sunday
Easy Run: 3–6 miles	*Mile Intervals*	*Easy Run:* 5–8 miles	*Alternate:* tempo/ hill/pace/ time-trial runs	*Easy Run:* 4–7 miles	*Rest!*	*Long Runs*

Make sure to bring along a stop watch to record your pace!

Mondays, Wednesdays, Fridays: Easy Runs

Easy runs are intended for recovery. Run these sessions at least thirty seconds per mile slower than your target marathon pace. In fact, sometimes I find it better to not wear a running watch on easy days.

As your training progresses, increase the length of your easy runs rather than the speed. When finished with an easy run you should feel refreshed—alternating an "easy" day with a "hard" day will give you more energy when you need it!

Tuesdays: Mile Intervals

Yep, more intervals—but these are a mile, and they need to be fast. Jog an easy quarter mile between each one to "rest."

Weeks One–Two: Do one day of (two) mile repeats at thirty seconds faster than your target marathon pace. So if your target pace is seven minutes a mile, you should run each of these at 6:30. If your target marathon pace is nine minutes a mile, you should run each of these at 8:30. This pace should stay the same for the rest of your mile-interval training.

Week Three: Add a mile to your repeats, for (three) mile repeats.

Weeks Four–Five: Now add two miles per session, so (five) mile repeats each week.

Weeks Six–Seven: If you're struggling, continue with five. If you're feeling good, up the number to (seven) mile repeats.

From here on out, add (two) mile repeats to your session every two weeks, until you max out at (thirteen) mile repeats per week. Hold this for the rest of your training—you may even want to decrease to (eleven) mile repeats—until about two weeks before the marathon.

Thursdays: Variety!

On Thursdays I offer a few different choices—pace runs, hill runs, tempo runs or time-trial runs. So many drills, I know! But don't get overwhelmed—choose whichever one feels right for your body that day. Who says we aren't flexible?

Pace Runs: Runs of ten to fifteen miles that you do at your target marathon pace.

Tempo Runs: These runs should be eight to twelve miles, increasing your mileage as you get closer to your marathon. For the first two miles of the run, take it easy as a warm-up. Then for miles three–ten kick it into gear, maintain a pace that's about fifteen seconds faster than your target marathon pace. So if your target marathon pace is seven minutes per mile, your pace here should be about 6:45. The last two miles should be a light cool-down.

Hill Runs: A tough variation on straight-up tempo runs—now, yes, on hills. These are a great way to gain strength and endurance. At the same time, they're tough on your legs, so avoid doing hill runs two weeks in a row.

Time Trial Runs: These can be of any distance. For the first half, run your target marathon pace. For the second half, "pick it up a bit"—at a pace that's fifteen seconds per mile faster. So if you're running ten miles total and your target marathon pace is eight minutes a mile, you'd run the first five miles at eight minutes a mile, and the second five at 7:45. This drill should be done at least every three or four weeks, and simulate what you should be trying to do in races—run negative splits!

Saturdays: Rest.

Woohoo!

Sundays: Long Runs

Start the first month with a twelve to fourteen mile long run and then increase by one or two miles per week every other week up to a maximum of twenty-two miles. Run them at an easy pace of a minute or a minute-and-a-half slower than your target marathon pace. So if your target marathon pace is seven minutes per mile, run these at an 8:00 or 8:30 pace.

Good running!

▼▼▼

9 The Triumph of Desire Over Reason

▼ ▼ ▼ ▼ ▼ ▼ ▼

The files are a dark, military green, each of them two inches thick, each stuffed with scraps of paper—news clippings, print-outs, certificates of completion—records of every single race, every single marathon I've ever run.

Scribbled on the frayed papers are notes in my languorous, slightly difficult-to-decipher handwriting. Notes about time, about finishing, about injuries, even about weather conditions: "Very hot, 85 degrees." "Major cramp, right calf." "16/400 in age group."

When files couldn't hold any more, I started using notebooks.

That was how, in November of 2000, I figured out that I had run exactly fifty-four marathons in my life. I did it as a lark, really, after my friend and assistant Carol asked me just how many I had done. I realized I had no idea.

I went home and pored over every scrap, every note, every entry, counting them one by one. There was Detroit in 1981, Boston in 1984, all the way past London in 2000—number 52.

And that was when I first thought, "Hmm. I bet I can reach 100."

Once I set that as a goal, I attacked. It had taken me almost twenty years to run fifty marathons. It would take only nine years to do the next forty-nine. In December of 2007, I ran Dallas—number 97. In January of 2008, just one month later, came Houston—98. Then number 99 in February, at Myrtle Beach.

I was packing them in because I knew exactly where I wanted my big one hundred to be: at the greatest, most historic marathon in the world—at Boston. Not only that, but I found out that

Boston would take place that year on Monday, April 21—my sixty-fifth birthday.

How cool is that?

It would be perfect—I would run it with Nelson Williams, one of my best friends and running buddies, and my whole family would be there to cheer me on, Jackie, my girlfriend, and my sons, Chris and Mike. In fact, there was just one thing standing between me and the realization of the greatest goal of my life: the simple fact that one day before the big race, I couldn't run even two miles, much less twenty-six.

A minor detail, right?

As soon as I found out that my 100th marathon was going to be in Boston on my birthday...well, I might as well admit it: I started telling everyone I knew. Not just family and friends and other runners, but virtually every single patient who came to my dental office didn't just get a filling or a veneer—they also got a big earful about my big race on my sixty-fifth birthday. Even the local press got word of the event, and the *Ann Arbor News* sent a photographer—yes, he may also have been a patient—to my house to snap some photos of me as I ran. Expectations were high—which was the way I liked it.

What I did not like was that I was starting to feel sick. Very sick.

I don't get sick often. Sure, my stomach can be sensitive, particularly when it encounters diabolical dairy products—like the infamous cream that nearly ruined my first Boston. But aside from that, I'm blessed with a strong constitution. Unfortunately, my usually strong constitution decided to break down completely at the worst time.

The first signs started on a Wednesday, twelve days before Boston, and the same day the photographer, Eli Garfunkel, took some pictures of me for the *News*. I could tell that something was off, but I couldn't put my finger on it. My flu was still but a glimmer in some virus's nucleic acid. No big deal, I figured. I had plenty of time before the race.

It was a quick downward spiral from there.

The next day I woke up at my usual time, five in the morning. The Arabic coffee I drank—Nelson's infamous "high-octane stuff"—didn't taste right, didn't give me its usual kick. My throat was dry and scratchy and I felt sluggish. I dragged all day long at the office, and what was worse, I had to fly to Kansas City that night for a dental lecture all day Friday. By the time I flew back to Michigan on Friday night, the combination of a bad hotel steak, a strange bed and incessant chatter with my well-intentioned dental brethren made a quick, one-day trip feel more like Lindbergh's crossing of the Atlantic.

I collapsed as soon as I got home. The next morning, Jackie asked me if I wanted to get together with her and some girl-friends at her house later that night. The answer was no—I could barely move, much less be social. I later found out that the "girlfriends" had been sixty of my best friends—all invited by Jackie for a surprise party to celebrate my birthday run. I was devastated to miss it—and to force her to call every single person to cancel. But I wasn't going anywhere.

I spent most of the next four days in bed. My body hurt, my throat was a mix of sand paper and needles, and I had a temperature of 102 degrees. This was not good, and I was starting to worry. Just five more days till Number 100.

On Thursday, the article on my upcoming run was published in the *Ann Arbor News*. The writer, Seth Gordon, had interviewed me (practically on my death bed), as well as Nelson and David Bach, for a big feature-length piece.

My 100th marathon was officially a part of the public record. There was no backing down now.

Thankfully I was finally starting to feel better—but just barely. I managed to go to work on Thursday, and got some rest before flying with Jackie to Boston later that night. Jackie is an authentic Bostonian, complete with accent, so we were going to spend some time with her family to get the full New England experience. Maybe drive in the "caah" to get some "chowdah." Chris and Mike were also coming into town for the occasion, and they flew in Saturday morning. We had found rooms at a little bed and breakfast, just blocks away from the finish line, called The Jewel on Newberry, run by an eccentric Mediterranean man and his son, who loved to do nothing better than talk. Which, unfortunately, was exactly what my throat didn't need.

Everything was set, I had less than three days to go—and I still couldn't sleep through an entire night, coughing and waking up constantly to clear the phlegm from my lungs. I tried getting extra sleep during the day, but even that didn't seem to help.

On April 20, the day before the marathon, the day before the race, I knew I had to try to limber up my legs. I hadn't even jogged for ten whole days, and I needed to know what I was up against. Jackie and I decided we'd run an easy five miles, just to make sure I didn't push myself too hard too soon.

I hardly made it past two.

My legs didn't have it. I could barely keep up with Jackie, and we weren't even running at a nine-minute pace. Later that day, while we were waiting to meet up with Nelson for lunch, Jackie asked the inevitable question:

"Have you considered not running the marathon?"

Up until that moment, I hadn't even considered that option. I had finished all my other marathons—even Grandma's, when I had to walk the entire thing—why couldn't I finish this one too? But at the same time, I was facing something completely new. I had dealt with off days, with the inevitable slowing down that comes with age, and even with excruciating injuries. But I had never tried to run a marathon feeling this sick. Like my body simply lacked the energy, the very will, it took to make it happen.

Maybe I should pull out? I was sick, horribly sick. Everyone would understand. Besides, there would be other races, other birthdays, other Bostons.

But the truth was—there would be no other 100.

"No," I said. It was my final answer.

▼▼▼

My alarm sounded at 5:45 A.M. I got out of bed, showered, put my clothes on, and pinned my number just below my shirt. Not just any shirt, but a tank top that two of my running friends had designed for me, with a slogan on the back: "Running Shoes: $100. Marathon Entry Fee: $110. Cost of Running My 100th Marathon on My 65th Birthday: Priceless."

And just in case that was too subtle for anyone, I added a note to the front myself: "JOHN. 100th Marathon. Today is My Birthday."

Given how bad I was feeling, I was starting to wonder whether I really wanted so much attention. Too late now.

I walked to the nearby Hilton to meet Nelson and David Bach, who was also running that day. We got on a bus to take us to the start, in Hopkinton. Normally at a time like this I'd be buzzing with energy, joking with Nelson and Dave, talking about injuries or discussing our strategy for the race, maybe even share notes with other runners. Instead, as soon as the bus pulled out—I passed out. Not a good sign, but I desperately needed every one of the thirty minutes of sleep I got.

When I woke up we were almost at our destination. The runners were making their final preparations—pinning their numbers on, tying their timing chips to their shoes, greasing themselves up with Vaseline, and using the tiny, stopped-up bathroom one last time. The whole bus reeked of a pungent combination of sweat, Vaseline, and shit. The first wave of runners, including Dave, left at 9:45 A.M. By the time my wave of runners was called at 10:30, I was ready to get the hell out of there.

Nelson and I walked to the start. With 13,000 runners in each wave, we were all grouped in separate corals. I was assigned to the first coral—an excellent position—but I wanted to run with my friend, so I joined Nelson's coral toward the back. The way I felt it really didn't matter where I started.

I waited for the gun to go off. The start of any marathon—but especially Boston—always crackles with electricity. People are yelling and screaming, high-fiving and cheering, all the positive energy that's been bottled up for hours about to be released.

But my energy felt different this time. A deep uncertainty hovered around me. I simply had no idea how the next four hours of my life were going to play out.

The gun fired. There were so many people clumped together that at first everyone was walking. All around me, the crackling energy was reaching its crescendo as runners managed to break away from the pack and take off. But all my years of experience—and foolishly fast starts—kept me level-headed and focused. I had to conserve energy, because I'd need every ounce of it later.

Nelson and I reached a moderate ten-minute pace and held it.

As bad as I felt physically, I got a huge burst of encouragement thanks to an unlikely source—my shirt. It was a huge success, way beyond expectation. Dozens and dozens of runners came up behind me and congratulated me, some of them in awe, some in plain disbelief. Several women asked me if I was really sixty-five. I had to lie and tell them I was.

Probably the biggest impact, though, came from my name in giant letters on the front of my jersey.

"John! John!! JOHN!!!" people screamed, sometimes chanting it in unison. In some areas, like Wellesley College—famous for its coeds—the noise was deafening. I loved it. But I think Nelson loved it even more. As I struggled to keep my ailing legs moving, he would shout at people on the sidelines and point at my shirt just to make sure I got my due—and that he got a very good laugh.

Technically, the first half of the marathon went well. We ran it in just under two hours, conservatively enough to maintain our reserves for the second half. But I could tell something was wrong. Usually the first half of a race is one of my favorite parts—I get into a rhythm, clicking one mile after another almost effortlessly. But this time I was already working hard for every single mile. Each one seemed like it was taking forever, each one felt like its own battle.

I didn't say anything to Nelson, because I wanted to stay positive, but after running together so many years he could sense my body language. He could tell I was struggling.

Despite all our efforts to run smart and pace ourselves, there was no second wind in the second half of the run. By mile sixteen I knew I was in trouble. Not only was my body weak, but my legs were cramping. Our nine-minute pace went out the window. I tried stopping and walking briefly at water stops to regain some energy, but I gave that up because the temptation to just keep walking was so incredibly strong.

I had walked a marathon before, of course, but this was different. In Grandma's I had just been dealing with an injury; here, my whole body felt like it was about to give. If I started walking, I might not even finish. And I had to finish. This was Boston. This was 100.

By mile twenty, it was clear I wouldn't complete this marathon in under four hours, if at all. I turned to Nelson and told him to go ahead without me. Maybe he could still salvage a decent time.

"Are you kidding?" he said incredulously. "You helped me get here. I'm gonna stay with you until we both cross the finish line."

What a friend. If he hadn't made that decision, I honestly don't know if I could've kept going. We kept at it, our pace getting slower and slower. Pretty soon, running turned into shuffling and shuffling turned into dragging my feet. I felt horrible and I probably looked worse. That didn't stop spectators from cheering us on—again, thanks to the mighty shirt.

"Go John!" they shouted. "Keep it up! You're almost there!"

That, of course, was a lie—we had four miles to go, but I tried not to think about it. For a short while a group of four or five young runners even ran with us, urging me on, pushing me forward. I looked at the leader and forced a smile.

"What I really need now is a fresh set of legs," I said. "Can I borrow yours?"

"Sure," he said. And just like that, they took off, gone.

We passed Boston University, meaning we had less than three miles to go. Usually I would be able to finish that in twenty minutes. Now, however, it was taking me twelve minutes to run a single mile. I told Nelson to go ahead of me. Again, he refused. And again, I thanked God for such a great friend.

I saw a shirt once—perhaps even more profound than the shirt I was wearing today—and it said, "Marathons: The Triumph of Desire Over Reason." Nothing I've ever read has so perfectly summed up what it means to me to be a marathoner. Think about it. Twenty-six and two-tenths miles from beginning to end. I don't care how good of shape you're in, does running that distance ever really make sense? Is there anything logical, anything reasonable, about putting your body through that kind of punishment?

Absolutely not. And that's entirely the point.

Why do we push ourselves to do anything, really? To develop a meaningful career and not just a job that gives us a regular paycheck? To build a strong family and friendships instead of simply being alone? Is there anything logical, anything reasonable, about the things that make our lives so special? That make them worth living?

Absolutely not. And that's entirely the point.

"Marathons: The Triumph of Desire Over Reason." You might as well just say that about life. It's just as true.

Nelson and I hit Commonwealth Boulevard—one of the last stretches, but one that seems to go on forever and ever. Nelson kept encouraging me the whole way. Soon we turned onto Hereford, the last street before Boylston. I noticed Steve's Breakfast Place, where Jackie, Nelson and I had eaten breakfast just a day earlier. Then we were on Boylston, and I could see a banner proclaiming "Boston Marathon Finish." I could hear Jackie and my sons, Mike and Chris, screaming my name, see them waving a sign about my 100th marathon, feel the crowds of thousands and thousands of people all around me, cheering.

It was surreal. Hallelujah.

I waved and kept running. Thirty yards, twenty, ten. And finally the finish line. My time was 4:19:30, but I don't know if a time has ever meant less to me.

I hugged Nelson, thanked him for staying with me the entire way. A race volunteer wrapped me in a space blanket that helped warm my exhausted body. I saw my family waiting for me on the sidelines. We embraced, and I felt faint, staggering against the metal railing as my face went pale, my eyes lost focus and the glare of the sun blinded me—miles and miles of pain and perseverance finally catching up with my ailing body.

"Dad, are you okay?" Chris asked. Jackie gave me her sunglasses and Mike moved quickly to get me some much-needed orange juice to restore my blood sugar.

After a few minutes of rest, my strength began to return. The hot shower I took back at the bed and breakfast may have been one of the greatest, most relieving experiences of my life. Now that it was all over with, my health improved incredibly quickly, the flu of the last two weeks disappearing almost immediately, as if in response to the huge milestone of running my 100th marathon finally being lifted from my shoulders.

I had done it. Finally. And I had to ask myself: Had it not been my 100th, had it not been Boston, had it not been my sixty-fifth birthday with all my family and friends rooting for me, would I have gone through with that race, given how sick I was? Hell no.

But it was over with. I had accomplished everything I had set out to do. And now that it was done, all I wanted to know was: when is number 101?

▼▼▼

▼ Nelson's Corner 9 ▼ My Own Thoughts on John's 100th Marathon.

Years ago, in 1995 I believe, while running with my friend John we were talking about everything runners talk about, solving world issues and comparing notes—he's probably mentioned that I love to talk. I was comparing notes to get the inside scoop on John's running, and I learned that he had run about forty marathons while I had four under my belt. He wasn't trying to impress me—in fact, he himself wasn't sure of the exact number.

On a whim, I blurted out that, when he got to his 100th marathon, I would run it with him. I was sure this was a promise I would never need to keep. Was I wrong!

Well, twelve years later, in late summer of 2007, we were running the last four hilly, character-building miles of what we call our North Campus Loop—some days I really hate this course, and today I was really struggling—when John casually told me that he planned on running number 100 in Boston the upcoming spring. It took a few minutes to register in my current state, but when it did I was shocked! By that point I had still only run sixteen marathons. The last one I had run was over a year ago, the Grandma's that John had to walk twenty-one miles to complete.

But I had made a promise and I had to keep it. First, I had to get into marathon running shape, then I had to run a 3:45 marathon to even qualify for Boston, and then I had to run Boston itself—all within less than a year. No problem, right?

My first try at qualifying came in Dallas, in the first week of December.I had only nine weeks to prepare, and I wasn't confident. Nevertheless, I was able to get in three long runs before the date of the race, I was feeling good and hoping for the best. Well, so much for that. On a cold, rainy, windy day—conditions that made the running much harder—I managed to miss the qualifying time by a measly forty-six seconds. Now what to do? I still had this promise hanging over me.

When I got home, I found out I had one last chance—Myrtle Beach in early February. I signed up for it immediately. If I didn't make this one, that was it—John was on his own in Boston. Thankfully, the Myrtle course is flat, the weather mild, and the size of the field small, with only about 2,500 runners. I had one marathon under my belt already, and most important, I had John himself at Myrtle Beach to help see me through. He and I can get into the zone when we run together, and I usually run better as a result.

On race day I was very confident. John and I positioned ourselves toward the front and we clicked mile after mile at an 8:30 pace. I felt great until about mile twenty-one, but with the temperature rising to the mid-sixties I started fading and losing concentration. But John stayed right by me. He kept encouraging me to hang in and maintain the pace. We slowed down to about nine minutes per mile, but we had a slight cushion to work with. At about mile twenty-four, I finally got myself back together and finished strong at 3:43. I had my qualifying time—I would be able to keep my promise. And I wouldn't forget how John had helped me do it.

As soon as I got home I signed up for Boston. The weekend of the race came and I flew to Massachusetts to meet up with John and Jackie. I knew John had been recovering from the flu, and

I was hoping he was over it so we could run together and enjoy the day. Unfortunately, though, when I met them for dinner Saturday night I could quickly tell that John wasn't his usual self. He was quiet and looked tired, but I didn't want to say anything. He still had one day to recover.

On race day, we boarded the bus for the start in Hopkinton—and John promptly fell asleep. That was very unusual for him. But he's a tough competitor whom I've learned never to underestimate, so I didn't give it much thought.

The race started, runners crammed into the narrow country road, with a lot of walking and trotting. As far as the eye could see, waves of colorful, festive people snaked their way through the pass. I felt pretty good and John seemed happy that the day had finally come. The weather was good for Boston. Cool with a breeze. No rain. We settled into a pace as we always do, and tried to stick with our plan—go out slowly at about a nine-minute pace and speed up later if all was well.

Halfway through the race I knew something wasn't right. Usually at this point John becomes more focused and works hard to keep the pace, even trying for "negative splits"—in other words, actually getting faster as the race progresses. Not on this day. We began to stop and walk at water stops, with the walks getting longer and longer. John was running on empty and we still had a third of the distance to go.

John encouraged me to go ahead. He knew I felt good, and he didn't want to hold me back. I couldn't do that to him. After all, he got me through not one but two attempts at qualifying for this race. How could I leave him now? What about my promise to run number 100 with him? I decided it was my turn to help him pull through a marathon.

I put on my most optimist face, turned to him and said, "I only wish I brought ear plugs along for these last few miles."

It was true—the crowd was screaming for us. Or more specifically, screaming for John and his fantastic shirt, which announced that it was both his birthday and his 100th marathon. John looked at me and smiled back.

As we got closer to the city, the crowd continued to swell—and to notice John's shirt. They were screaming, encouraging and congratulating John from both sides of the road. I was feeling the energy, proud to be running alongside him. But John was struggling, almost as if someone had pulled a plug and drained all his energy. I've never seen him that way. I wasn't even sure he would make it to the finish.

But he persisted, slowly dragging one foot after the other, inching his way from Commonwealth towards Hereford Street.

"Hey," I said. "Let's try to look good finishing."

As usual, he somehow began to pick it up a bit—and we crossed the line together. It was a challenging run, more challenging than either of us could have anticipated. John really put it all on the line for that race. I never expected anything less from him.

▼▼▼

I have now been running for more than forty years, amassing a total of over 400 races and 80,000 miles. Am I still passionate about running? Do I still have fire in the belly? Has Mother Nature been kind?

Yes, yes and yes.

I love to run. I love to run races. I love the excitement of standing with hordes of people anticipating the sound of the starting signal. I love to size up runners, especially those who might be in my age group. Does he look fast? Is that someone I can stay with?

I love running on the edge. Pacing myself so I push hard, yet still have enough in the tank when I need it at the finish. Nelson, with yet another wise Nelsonism, even told Dave Bach that "at the end of a race, if you're close to John, you're toast."

That said, I love winning—it is rewarding—but that is not the reason I run.

I run because I love people, I love connecting with people—before, during and after races. I don't like it when runners wear ear phones and are totally zoned out, or even worse when they're bothered if you try talking to them. They're not just missing out on other runners, they're missing out on the sounds of nature. Birds greeting the early morning hours, leaves rustling in the wind and even the melodic croaks of frogs in the early spring. No music can come close.

I run because I like to get the best performance out of my body on that day, in that moment. I like it when my body feels like a well-oiled machine, firing on all cylinders.

But I have to admit that staying in that kind of shape is getting harder and harder as I age. It takes much more effort to achieve much lower results, and it's a lot easier to get injured—call it the "law of diminishing returns." As I often tell friends, "My head tells me I can run faster, but my body doesn't go along."

Look at my times in races over the past thirty years in *Nuts and Bolts* under "Performance Puzzle" and you'll see that the trend is clear: I'm getting slower.

Does that discourage me? No. I still possess the desire. I still have *la joie de courir*. I am an eternal optimist.

In March 2011, I was snowboarding in Aspen and I injured my groin. And actually, I wasn't even snowboarding at the time—I was just getting in line for the ski lift.

Because of my injury, I reset my sights on my running career. In July, I went with Stan Watson to Glen Arbor, Michigan, for a short weekend trip. (Remember Stan? I used to throw stones at his window to wake him up for runs back in our college days.) I signed up for a race in nearby Leland—The Fishtown 5K—and talked Stan into signing up too.

The morning of the race it was hot and humid. There weren't many runners there, maybe 200 entries of all ages—even including some kids—mostly from families vacationing in the area. Stan and I lined up towards the back, happy to let all the anxious runners sprint ahead of us. Stan hadn't been running much and decided to walk it barefoot since he hadn't even brought his running shoes. I wanted to run an easy eight-minute pace—just enjoy my surroundings, talk to some people and hopefully not aggravate my injury.

Despite my plan, at mile one I started to gradually pass people, not because I was speeding up but more because so many of the unseasoned runners were slowing down, especially the younger kids. It reminded me of my first race in Boy Scouts.

I talked to some people and encouraged them. They were struggling and sweating in the heat, and at that point most of them just wanted to finish. I was struggling too, much more than usual—the weather was brutal. With two tenths of a mile to go I came upon a boy who was walking, he couldn't have been older than ten, his face beet red and frustration written all over it.

"Come on," I said. "You are almost there, stay with me, you can make it."

I literally tapped him on the shoulder to get him moving. Sure enough, he started running. We ran side by side—he was huffing and puffing and I kept telling him to keep going. We were about thirty yards from the finish when he took off, sprinting as fast as he could to beat me.

For once, I did not pick it up a bit.

He smoked me. When I finished, he was standing just beyond the finish line with a huge grin on his face.

"See?" I said, "You did a great job and had an awesome finish!"

He just smiled and I felt good.

I waited around for Stan, who finished in forty-one minutes with sore feet, blistered and blackened from the pavement. He too had a big smile. It was his first race in five years. He's had some heart issues that have definitely slowed him down.

"Good job, Stan," I said, and we high-fived it.

Stan was happy he ran the race. The time was not important.

I feel very fortunate to have friends like Stan and Nelson, Bob and Dave. Just like running, friends make my life more meaningful, fulfilling and healthy. What more do I need?

I turned to Stan and said, "Okay, let's go find that place in Northpoint and have breakfast."

▼▼▼

Appendix: Nuts and Bolts
▼ ▼ ▼ ▼ ▼ ▼ ▼

Performance Puzzle

As of late, Nelson and I have noticed that our times are not as fast as they used to be. It sucks that we are slower. Doesn't sound all that surprising for two guys who have been running for over thirty years, does it?

Nelson will say, "Remember when we used to run this loop ten minutes faster?"

"I sure do," I reply. "It's an eight-mile loop, for God's sake. Why are we so slow"?

My head tells me I can run faster but my body does not go along. What is happening here?

Bluntly put, we are older. But what is it about the aging process that causes runners to slow down? Can we get some of the speed and endurance back?

To gain some insight, I decided to review all the data I had on my running going back to 1980. Nelson, totally independently, has also kept a daily diary since we met in 1991. Some of his entries have little to do with running but more to with the events accompanying each run, but it was still interesting reviewing our evolution as runners.

I tabulated 416 races that I ran over the past thirty years and averaged my finishing times in the 10K, the ten-mile run, the half marathon and the full marathon (Table 1). I averaged my times in each category over a five-year intervals and plotted them in Figures 1 and 2. The slowdown in each category is very clear. It is especially noticeable the last ten years. Sure, some of the slowdown is due simply to an increase in the number and frequency of my long-distance races. But much of it is due purely to aging (Figure 3). Table 2 highlights my PR times for various distances.

What can a runner do to halt this slide? Nelson and I calculated that, with the right training, on average a runner should be able to improve his/her time by eight to ten percent over a period of six months. For example, if you are a four-hour marathoner, you should be able to get down to a 3:40 marathon with the proper training.

In the pages that follow we have provided you with several potential training schedules. Select the one that best fits your goals and get started. Always remember the three I's:

Individualize: Every person's fitness level is different and the body reacts differently to a given training regimen. Knowing your present level of fitness is crucial. Make sure your plan fits your goals.

Intensity: You can't run every day with the same intensity. Intensity depends on factors such as your training frequency, stress level, time availability, the amount of rest you've had, and even your eating habits. Take these factors into account as you prepare to run each day. If it feels difficult that day, don't be disappointed, you are still benefiting from your training.

Inconsistency: Of course, you need to maintain some regularity. Running seven days one week and two days the next is not a good way to improve. That said, you also don't want to get stuck in a rut. Vary your distance, terrain, pace, and course. Find new people to run with. This will keep things fresh and keep you motivated.

By now you may be saying to yourself, "Sure, it's easy for these guys to give advice—they've been running forever. But what about a beginner like me?" Trust me, nothing ever comes easy—even for the most experienced runners. Running is similar to climbing a mountain; there is a constant ebb and flow. You're always trying to reach the peak, but sometimes you have to descend a little to reach a safer route. It's not a straight line progression. But once you reach the top, there's no greater reward. The ultimate goal here is not just to run a race in a certain time but to achieve and maintain an overall level of health, fitness and well-being for a lifetime—regardless of your age.

You need a minimum of four hours per week to establish a baseline for fitness. At least half of that time should be spent running while the balance could be spent walking, spinning, lifting weights or doing yoga. Once you're ready to attain a mid-level fitness standard, double your training time per week to eight hours. Do it gradually over a three-month period. If you like to perform at an even higher plateau you need to triple your weekly training time. Investing twelve hours a week for regular training and exercise requires commitment and persistence—but the rewards are endless.

I call this John's 4/8/12 rule for fitness.

For more information see our web site:

www.letspickitupabit.com

▼▼▼

Table 1. Average Race Times Over 30 Years

Year	10K	10 mi	Half	Marathon
1981–1985	38.7	62.7	84.0	192
1986–1990	38.0	61.4	83.1	194
1991–1995	39.3	64.5	84.7	200
1996–2000	40.3	66.6	87.8	201
2001–2005	42.0	68.8	92.0	212
2006–2010	46.5	73.8	102.0	233

Table 2. Personal Records

Distance	No. of Races	PR Time	Pace/Mile
5K	7	17:20	5:35
10K	102	36:10	5:50
10 mi	59	59:45	5:58
20K	20	1:17:40	6:15
Half Marathon	57	1:18:54	6:00
25K	24	1:37:20	6:15
Marathon	121	3:02:00	6:57

Figure 1: Average Race Times Over 30 Years: Half Marathon, 10 Mi, 10K

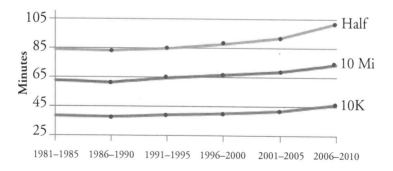

Figure 2. Average Race Times Over 30 Years: Marathon

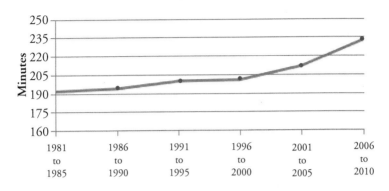

Figure 3. Percent Increase in Race Times as a Function of Age

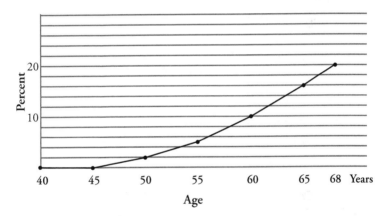

▼▼▼

An Explanation of the Training Schedules

The tables in this section are intended to be guidelines you can use to train for a variety of common distance races. Notice that there are three "goal paces" shown for each race distance. Select the pace chart that best fits your experience and fitness level. These training programs run for sixteen weeks. If you are already running more than twenty miles per week, you can start your program at the week most closely matching your current level.

Always take into account how your body is adapting, and make adjustments to distance and intensity. Learning to "listen to your body" is perhaps the most important (and most often ignored) aspect of training.

Some of the terms used in the charts are:

Easy run days. Pace yourself at about one and a half to two minutes/mile slower than your 5K race pace. If you haven't done a 5K race, run slowly enough that you can cover the required distance and feel refreshed, not exhausted, at the end.

Tempo run days: Pace yourself about one min/mile slower than your 5K race pace. Obviously, tempo runs are going to be harder, so they are typically done just once/week.

Long run days: Pace yourself as on the light run days. You will be running two–three times farther, so adjust pace accordingly. There is no shame in walking part of a long run, especially if you are just staring a running program. The important thing is to cover the distance, and get used to being on your feet for a longer period of time.

Speed workout day: Each chart shows speed workouts on Tuesdays. Make it any day you want, just not the day before the long run! Try to find a local school track for these workouts. All of the workouts described are called "repeats," with the rest in between the "interval." Warm up thoroughly before attempting a speed workout. We recommend jogging at least a mile. Rest intervals between most repeats are 400m. Walking the rest interval between repeats is OK, but continuing to jog even very slowly, is actually better. This keeps your heart rate higher, improving recovery. Pace yourself. If you are scheduled to do 6×400m, don't spend all your energy on the first one! Try instead to run each successive repeat slightly faster than the one before. If you have too much energy left on the last one, adjust your pace accordingly next session. Finally, try to be consistent doing the speed work sessions. You will make progress much more quickly, and be less likely to be injured.

Tapering: This is a technique used by most successful runners. It means gradually reducing your training mileage over the last ten to twelve days before a big race. Each chart shows how to effectively reduce mileage so your tank is full on race day.

▼▼▼

Table 3—5K Goal Pace: 10 min/mi—16 Week Plan

Week	Mon	Tues	Wed	Thurs	Fri	Sat	Sun	TOTAL
1	3	4×200m (200m rests)	3	0	3	0	6	15
2	4	5×200m (200m rests)	3	0	5	4	6	22
3	3	6×200m (200m rests)	4	3	0	0	6	16
4	0	3×400m (400m rests)	3	4	0	3	7	17
5	3	8×200m (200m rests)	6	0	3	0	8	20
6	4	4×400m (400m rests)	3	5	3	0	7	22
7	4	8×200m (200m rests)	3	0	3	3	8	21
8	3	4×400m (400m rests)	4	4	0	3	7	21
9	6	6×200m (200m rests)	4	5	0	0	8	23
10	4	6×400m (400m rests)	3	6	3	3	7	26
11	4	8×200m (200m rests)	3	4	0	0	8	19
12	4	8×400m (400m rests)	4	6	0	4	8	26
13	0	12×200m (200m rests)	0	4	4	3	8	19
14	5	2×800m (400m rests)	3	5	4	0	8	25
15	4	10×200m (200m rests)	3	4	0	4	7	22
16	0	3	0	3	0	0	RACE	6

Pace Codes

M, W, F, S—Light: 11.5–12.5 min/mi	Tu—Speed: 9–9.5 min/mi	Th—Tempo: 11–11.5 min/mi	Su—Long Run: 12-13 min/mi

Note: Speed workout distance is not included in total weekly mileage. "m"=meters for speed workout. Week 16 is easy week with weekend race.

Table 4—5K Goal Pace: 8 min/mi—16 Week Plan

Week	Mon	Tues	Wed	Thurs	Fri	Sat	Sun	TOTAL
1	3	6×200m (200m rests)	3	0	3	0	6	15
2	4	8×200m (200m rests)	3	0	5	4	6	22
3	3	10×200m (200m rests)	4	3	0	0	7	17
4	0	12×200m (200m rests)	3	6	0	3	7	19
5	3	12×200m (200m rests)	6	0	3	0	8	20
6	4	4×400m (400m rests)	3	6	3	0	7	23
7	4	10×200m (200m rests)	3	0	3	3	8	21
8	3	6×400m (400m rests)	4	6	0	3	9	25
9	6	12×200m (200m rests)	4	6	0	0	8	24
10	4	8×400m (400m rests)	4	6	3	3	10	30
11	4	10×400m (400m rests)	3	4	0	0	9	20
12	4	12×400m (400m rests)	4	6	0	4	10	28
13	0	14×200m (400m rests)	0	6	4	3	9	22
14	6	6×800m (400m rest)	4	6	4	0	12	32
15	6	8×800m (400m rest)	3	4	0	4	10	27
16	4	3	0	3	0	0	RACE	10

Pace Codes

M, W, F, S—Light: 8.5–9.5 min/mi	Tu—Speed: 7–7.5 min/mi	Th—Tempo: 7.5–8 min/mi	Su—Long Run: 8–9 min/mi

Note: Speed workout distance is not included in total weekly mileage. "m" =meters for speed workout. Week 16 is easy week with weekend race.

Table 5—5K Goal Pace: 6 min/mi—16 Week Plan

Week	Mon	Tues	Wed	Thurs	Fri*	Sat	Sun	TOTAL
1	4	6×200m (200m rests)	3	0	4×400m	4	10	21
2	6	8×200m (200m rests)	3	0	6×400m	0	12	21
3	3	2× (400m, 400m, 200m, 600m) (400m rests)	4	6	8×400m	6	10	29
4	0	800m, 600m, 400m 200m 400m 600m, 800m (400m rests)	4	6	8×400m	3	12	25
5	3	14×200m (200m rests)	4	0	10×400m	4	10	21
6	4	3×1600m (400m rests)	3	8	6×400m	4	12	31
7	6	10×800m (400m rests)	3	0	7×400m	3	14	26
8	3	3× (400m, 400m, 200m, 600m) (400m rests)	4	6	8×400m	0	12	25
9	6	800m, 600m, 400m, 200m, 400m, 600m, 800m, 600m, 400m, 200m (400m rests)	4	6	9×400m	0	14	30
10	8	16×200m (200m rests)	4	8	10×400	5	12	37
11	0	4×1600m (400m rests)	5	8	8×400	4	14	31
12	3	12×800m (400m rests)	6	8	12×400m	4	12	33
13	0	4× (400m, 400m, 200m, 600m) (400m rests)	4	8	10×400m	4	14	30
14	6	1200m, 800m, 600m, 400m, 200m, 400m, 600m, 800m, 1200m (400m rests)	4	8	12×400m	5	12	35
15	6	14×200m (200m rests)	3	6	10×400m	5	10	30
16	4	3	5	3	0	0	RACE	15

Pace Codes

M, W, S—Light: 8–8.5 min/mi	Tu, F—Speed: 5.5–6.5 min/mi	Th—Tempo: 7–7.5 min/mi	Su—Long Run: 7–8.0 min/mi

Notes: Speed workout distance is not included in total weekly mileage. "m" =meters for speed workout. Week 16 is easy week with weekend race.
* 200m rests for all Friday workouts

Table 6—10K Goal Pace: 10 min/mi—16 Week Plan

Week	Mon	Tues	Wed	Thurs	Fri	Sat	Sun	TOTAL
1	3	2×400m (200m rests)	3	0	3	0	8	17
2	4	2×800m (400m rests)	3	0	5	0	4	16
3	3	1× (400m, 400m, 200m, 600m) (400m rests)	4	3	3	0	8	21
4	0	800m, 600m, 400m, 200m (200m rests)	4	4	3	0	9	20
5	3	4×400m (400m rests)	4	0	3	0	8	18
6	4	2×1600m (400m rests)	3	4	3	0	9	23
7	6	4×800m (400m rests)	3	0	4	0	8	21
8	3	2× (400m, 400m, 200m, 600m) (400m rests)	4	3	5	0	9	24
9	6	800m, 600m, 2×400m, 2×200m (400m rests)	4	3	0	0	8	21
10	4	8×400m (400m rests)	4	3	3	0	9	23
11	4	2×1600m (400m rests)	3	4	3	0	9	23
12	4	4×800m (400m rests)	4	5	3	0	8	24
13	3	3× (400m, 400m, 200m, 600m) (400m rests)	6	4	4	0	9	26
14	6	800m, 800m, 400m, 200m (200m rests)	4	5	4	0	8	27
15	4	8×400m (400m rests)	3	5	3	0	7	22
16	3	3	0	3	0	0	RACE	9

Pace Codes

M, W, F, S—Light: 11.5–12.5 min/mi	Tu—Speed: 9–9.5 min/mi	Th—Tempo: 11–11.5 min/mi	Su—Long Run: 12–13 min/mi

Notes: Speed workout distance is not included in total weekly mileage. "m" = meters for speed workout. Week 16 is easy week with weekend race.

131

Table 7—10K Goal Pace: 8 min/mi—16 Week Plan

Week	Mon	Tues	Wed	Thurs	Fri	Sat	Sun	TOTAL
1	3	6×400m (400m rests)	3	0	3	3	8	20
2	4	4×800m (400m rests)	3	3	6	0	4	20
3	3	1× (400m, 400m, 200m, 600m) (400m rests)	4	6	0	3	10	26
4	0	800m, 600m, 400m, 200m (200m rests)	4	6	0	2	9	21
5	3	6×400m (200m rests)	4	0	5	3	10	25
6	5	2×1600m (400m rests)	3	6	4	0	10	28
7	5	6×800m (400m rests)	3	0	6	3	8	25
8	5	2× (400m, 400m, 200m, 600m) (400m rests)	4	7	0	4	10	30
9	6	800m (400m rest); 600m (200m rest); 2×400m (200m rests), 2×200m (100m rests)	3	6	4	0	9	28
10	6	8×400m (200m rests)	5	6	3	5	10	35
11	5	7×800m (400m rests)	3	6	3	3	10	30
12	5	4×1600m (400m rests)	5	6	4	6	9	35
13	4	3× (400m, 400m, 200m, 600m) (400m rests)	6	7	4	4	10	35
14	6	1200m, 800m, 600m, 2×400m, 4×200m (200m rests)	4	7	4	0	10	31
15	6	10×400m (200m rests)	4	5	4	0	8	27
16	3	5	3	3	0	0	RACE	14

Pace Codes

M, W, F, S—Light: 8.5–9.5 min/mi	Tu—Speed: 7–7.5 min/mi	Th—Tempo: 7.5–8 min/mi	Su—Long Run: 8–9 min/mi

Notes: Speed workout distance is not included in total weekly mileage. "m"=meters for speed workout. Week 16 is easy week with weekend race.

Table 8—10K Goal Pace: 6 min/mi—16 Week Plan

Week	Mon	Tues	Wed	Thurs	Fri*	Sat	Sun	TOTAL
1	3	2×1600m (400m rests)	5	3	4×400m	4	8	23
2	4	4×800m (400m rests)	3	5	6×400m	5	9	26
3	3	1×(400m, 400m, 200m, 600m) (400m rests)	4	6	8×400m	0	10	23
4	4	800m, 600m, 400m, 200m (400m rests)	4	7	8×400m	4	9	28
5	5	6×400m (400m rests)	4	0	10×400m	0	12	21
6	4	3×1600m (400m rests)	3	8	6×400m	5	10	30
7	6	6×800m (400m rests)	3	3	7×400m	0	11	23
8	5	2×(400m, 400m, 200m, 600m) (400m rests)	5	6	8×400m	5	10	31
9	6	800m (400m rest); 600m (400m rest) 2×400m, 2×200m (200m rests)	4	8	9×400m	4	12	34
10	5	8×400m (200m rests)	4	6	10×400m	0	10	25
11	4	4×1600m (400m rests)	5	8	10×400m	6	14	37
12	4	8×800m (400m rests)	4	8	12×400m	4	10	30
13	6	3×(400m, 400m, 200m, 600m) (400m rests)	6	9	14×400m	5	12	38
14	6	1200m, 800m, 600m, 2×400m, 4×200m (200m rests)	6	8	12×400m	3	16	39
15	5	10×400m (200m rests)	6	7	10×400m	4	10	32
16	3	5	3	5	3	0	RACE	19

Pace Codes

M, W, F, S—Light: 8–8.5 min/mi	Tu—Speed: 5.5–6.5 min/mi	Th—Tempo: 7–7.5 min/mi	Su—Long Run: 7–8.0 min/mi

Notes: Speed workout distance is not included in total weekly mileage. "m"=meters for speed workout. Week 16 is easy week with weekend race.
*200m rests for all Friday workouts.

133

Table 9—Half Marathon Goal Pace: 10 min/mi—16 Week Plan

Week	Mon	Tues	Wed	Thurs	Fri	Sat	Sun	TOTAL
1	3	2×800m (400m rests)	3	0	3	0	6	15
2	4	4×800m (400m rests)	3	0	5	0	6	18
3	3	1× (400m, 400m, 200m, 600m) (400m rests)	4	3	0	0	7	17
4	3	800m, 600m, 400m, 200m (200m rests)	3	6	0	0	7	19
5	3	6×400m (200m rests)	6	0	3	0	8	20
6	4	2×1600m (400m rests)	3	6	3	0	7	23
7	4	4×800m (200m rests)	3	0	3	3	8	21
8	3	2× (400m, 400m, 200m, 600m) (400m rests)	4	6	0	3	9	25
9	6	800m, 600m, 2×400m, 2×200m (200m rests)	4	6	0	0	8	24
10	4	8×400m (200m rests)	4	6	3	3	10	30
11	4	2×1600m (400m rests)	3	4	0	0	9	20
12	4	6×800m (400m rests)	4	6	0	4	11	29
13	0	2× (400m, 400m, 200m, 600m) (400m rests)	0	4	4	3	9	20
14	6	2× (1200m, 400m rest; 800m, 200m rest; 600m, 200m rest)	4	4	4	0	12	30
15	6	8×400m (200m rests)	3	4	6	0	10	29
16	3	3	0	3	0	0	RACE	9

Pace Codes

M, W, F, S—Light: 11.5-12.5 min/mi	Tu—Speed: 9-9.5 min/mi	Th—Tempo: 11-11.5 min/mi	Su—Long Run: 12-13 min/mi

Notes: Speed workout distance is not included in total weekly mileage. "m"=meters for speed workout. Week 16 is easy week with weekend race.

Table 10—Half Marathon Goal Pace: 8 min/mi—16 Week Plan

Week	Mon	Tues	Wed	Thurs	Fri	Sat	Sun	TOTAL
1	3	4×800m (400m rests)	3	0	3	4	9	22
2	4	6×800m (400m rests)	3	0	5	0	10	22
3	3	2× (800m, 400m, 200m, 600m) (400m rests)	4	6	0	3	10	26
4	0	2× (800m, 600m, 400m, 200m) (200m rests)	4	6	0	3	9	22
5	3	8×400m (200m rests)	4	0	3	0	12	22
6	4	2×1600m (400m rests)	3	6	3	4	10	30
7	6	4×800m (200m rests)	3	6	3	0	8	26
8	4	2× (400m, 200m rest; 400m, 200m rest; 200m, 100m rest; 600m, 200m rest)	4	6	3	0	10	27
9	6	800m (400m rest); 600m (400m rest); 2×400m (200m rests); 2×200m (100m rests)	4	6	4	4	12	36
10	4	8×400m (200m rests)	4	6	3	5	10	32
11	4	3×1600m (400m rests)	3	6	4	6	14	37
12	4	8×800m (400m rests)	4	8	6	4	10	36
13	0	2× (400m, 400m, 200m, 600m) (400m rests)	6	6	4	4	12	32
14	6	3× (1200m, 400m rest; 800m, 200m rest; 600m, 200m rest)	4	6	4	5	12	37
15	6	10×400m (200m rests)	6	7	4	6	10	39
16	3	4	0	3	0	0	RACE	10

Pace Codes

M, W, F, S—Light: 8.5–9.5 min/mi	Tu—Speed: 7–7.5 min/mi	Th—Tempo: 7.5–8 min/mi	Su—Long Run: 8–9 min/mi

Notes: Speed workout distance is not included in total weekly mileage. "m" =meters for speed workout. Week 16 is easy week with week-

135

Table 11—Half Marathon Goal Pace: 6.5 min/mi—16 Week Plan

Week	M	Tues	W	Ths	F*	S	Su	TOTAL
1	4	8×800m (400m rests)	3	3	4×400m	4	10	24
2	6	3×1600m	3	5	6×400m	4	9	27
3	3	2×(400m, 400m, 200m, 600m) (400m rests)	5	5	8×400m	6	12	31
4	3	800m, 600m, 400m, 200m, 200m, 400m, 600m, 800m (400m rests)	4	6	8×400m	0	15	28
5	3	10×400m (200m rests)	4	0	10×400m	4	12	23
6	4	5×1600m (400m rests)	3	8	6×400m	4	15	34
7	6	10×800m (400m rests)	3	0	7×400m	3	12	24
8	5	3×(400m, 200m rest; 400m, 200m rest; 200m, 100m rest; 600m, 200m rest)	4	6	8×400m	0	16	31
9	6	800m, 600m, 400m, 200m, 400m, 600m, 800m, 600m, 400m, 200m, (200m rests)	4	6	9×400m	3	14	33
10	6	12×400m (200m rests)	6	8	10×400m	3	16	39
11	3	8×1600m (400m rests)	5	8	10×400m	4	12	32
12	5	12×800m (400m rests)	6	10	12×400m	4	15	40
13	0	4×(400m, 400m, 200m, 600m) (200m rests)	6	8	14×400m	6	14	34
14	4	1200m, 800m, 600m, 600m, 400m, 200m, 400m, 600m, 800m, 1200m (400m rests)	6	10	16×400	3	15	38
15	6	12×400m (200m rests)	4	6	12×400m	5	12	33
16	4	5	0	3	0	0	RACE	12

Pace Codes

M, W, S—Light: 8–8.5 min/mi	Tu, F—Speed: 5.5–6.5 min/mi	Th—Tempo: 7–7.5 min/mi	Su—Long Run: 7.5–8.0 min/mi

Notes: Speed workout distance is not included in total weekly mileage. "m" =meters for speed workout. Week 16 is easy week with weekend race.
*200m rests for all Friday workouts.

Table 12—Marathon Goal Pace: 10 min/mi—16 Week Plan

Week	Mon	Tues	Wed	Thurs	Fri	Sat	Sun	TOTAL
1	3	4×400m, 2×800m, 4×400m	4	3	3	0	10	23
2	4	6×800m	5	0	4	0	12	25
3	0	2× (400m, 400m, 200m, 600m) (400m rests)	6	4	6	0	12	28
4	0	2× (800m, 600m, 400m, 200m) (200m rests)	8	4	3	0	10	25
5	3	8×400m (200m rests)	9	4	5	0	12	33
6	4	5×1600m (400m rests)	10	5	7	0	13	39
7	6	8×800m (400m rests)	11	5	8	0	14	44
8	4	2× (400m, 400m, 200m, 600m) (400m rests)	12	5	8	0	16	45
9	6	2× (800m, 600m, 2×400m, 2×200m) (200m rests)	12	5	8	0	15	46
10	4	8×400m (200m rests)	11	5	8	0	16	44
11	4	5×1600m (400m rests)	12	6	4	0	20	46
12	4	8×800m (200m rests)	10	6	10	0	18	48
13	0	3× (400m, 400m, 200m, 600m) (400m rests)	12	5	11	0	16	44
14	6	1200m, 800m, 600m, 400m, 200m (200m rests)	10	3	6	0	14	39
15	6	10×400m (200m rests)	6	3	3	3	10	31
16	4	4	0	3	0	0	RACE	11

Pace Codes

M, W, F, S—Light: 11.5–12.5 min/mi	Tu—Speed: 9–9.5 min/mi	Th—Tempo: 11–11.5 min/mi	Su—Long Run: 12–13 min/mi

Notes: Speed workout distance is not included in total weekly mileage. "m"=meters for speed workout. Week 16 is easy week with weekend race.

Table 13—Marathon Goal Pace: 8 min/mi—16 Week Plan

Week	Mon	Tues	Wed	Thurs	Fri	Sat	Sun	TOTAL
1	3	4×400m, 2×800m, 4×400m	4	3	3	0	10	23
2	4	6×800m	5	0	4	0	12	25
3	0	2× (400m, 400m, 200m, 600m) (400m rests)	6	4	6	0	12	28
4	0	2× (800m, 600m, 400m, 200m)	8	4	3	0	10	25
5	3	8×400m	9	4	5	0	12	33
6	4	5×1600m	10	5	7	0	13	39
7	6	8×800m	11	5	8	3	14	47
8	4	3× (400m, 400m, 200m, 600m) (400m rests)	12	5	8	3	16	48
9	6	2× (800m, 600m, 2×400m, 2×200m)	12	5	7	3	16	49
10	4	10×400m	12	5	8	3	15	47
11	4	6×1600m	10	6	6	3	20	49
12	4	10×800m	10	6	8	3	18	49
13	0	4× (400m, 400m, 200m, 600m) (400m rests)	12	5	11	3	20	51
14	6	1200m, 800m, 600m, 2×400m 4×200m	10	3	6	3	12	40
15	6	12×400m	6	3	0	3	10	28
16	4	5	0	3	0	0	RACE	12

Pace Codes

M, W, F, S—Light: 8.5–9.5 min/mi	Tu—Speed: 7–7.5 min/mi	Th—Tempo: 7.5–8 min/mi	Su—Long Run: 8–9 min/mi

Notes: Speed workout distance is not included in total weekly mileage. "m"=meters for speed workout. Week 16 is easy week with weekend race.

Table 14—Marathon Goal Pace: 7 min/mi—16 Week Plan

Week	Mon	Tues	Wed	Thurs	Fri	Sat	Sun	TOTAL
1	3	4×400m, 2×800m, 4×400m (200m rests)	4	3	3	0	13	26
2	4	6×800m (200m rests)	5	0	4	0	12	25
3	0	2× (400m, 400m, 200m, 600m) 400m rests	6	4	6	0	15	31
4	0	2× (800m, 600m, 400m, 200m) (200m rests)	8	4	3	0	14	29
5	3	8×400m (200m rests)	9	4	5	0	16	37
6	4	5×1600m (400m rests)	10	5	7	0	17	43
7	6	8×800m (400m rests)	11	5	8	0	15	45
8	4	3× (400m, 400m, 200m, 600m) (400m rests)	12	5	8	0	20	49
9	6	2× (800m, 600m, 400m, 200m) (200m rests)	12	5	8	0	16	47
10	4	10×400m (200m rests)	13	5	8	0	20	50
11	4	6×1600m (400m rests)	13	6	9	3	16	51
12	4	10×800m (200m rests)	13	6	11	3	22	59
13	0	8×1600m (400m rests)	12	7	11	3	18	51
14	6	1200m, 800m, 600m, 400m, 200m (200m rests)	10	3	6	3	16	44
15	4	12×400m(200m rests)	6	4	3	3	12	32
16	4	5	0	4	0	0	RACE	13

Pace Codes

M, W, S—Light: 8.0–8.5 min/mi	Tu, F—Speed: 5.5–6.5 min/mi	Th—Tempo: 6.5–7.5 min/mi	Su—Long Run: 7–8 min/mi

Notes: Speed workout distance is not included in total weekly mileage. "m" =meters for speed workout. Week 16 is easy week with weekend race.

Acknowledgements and Thanks
▼ ▼ ▼ ▼ ▼ ▼

There are many individuals I would like to thank for contributing to this book— both in its telling and in its living.

First, my family: My sons, Christopher and Michael, have been with me from my first race in Florida to the present. Their unwavering support helped shape my life as a runner and father. My wife, Jackie, has provided constant encouragement. Her energy and incisive commentary has been instrumental in much more than just this book. My brothers and sisters, Gisele, Alice, Nelly, Francois and Emile, and my brother-in-law George Farah, have all been a crucial part of my life. They've always been there for me, and of course for my many Crim races in Flint. Gretchen Farah's steady hand and consistent care helped raise two honest, hardworking and caring young men in Christopher and Michael. Theresa Stanko also did a great job helping raise Christopher and Michael, and she'll always be an important part of my running world.

My best friends and running buddies: My longtime breakfast club, Stan Watson, Heinz Grassl, Stan Mendenhall, Ron Yapp, Dick Weber, John Powers, Badie Farah and Ted Beimel, have patiently listened to my exploits as a runner for the past forty years and always saved me a seat at the table. My first early-morning running buddy, John Shamraj, is a good friend and was on time most of the time. My tenacious 5:15 A.M. running partners, Bob Marty and Nelson Williams, have never failed me irrespective of weather conditions. You cannot find a tougher runner than Bob and a more creative, lively and talkative runner than Nelson. Dave Bach is unquestionably my steadiest and toughest Potawatomi Trail running buddy, and he's always up for a challenge. Along with Dave, my teammates in the "Dances with Dirt" relay races, Steve Bolling, Sharlene Day and Brad Dyke, have made every race challenging, interesting and memorable. Another Dave, Dave Ballou, has been both a dear friend and a tough-as-nails competitor for the past forty years in sailing, running and skiing. Not only that, but his zest for life on the dance floor is infectious and unequalled.

The rest of my support team: Jeff Barnett's astute guidance and personalized training helped me recover from numerous running injuries, allowing me to persevere in my quest. Bill Gregory gave great advice for my first marathon—go out easy, the race starts at mile twenty—which I promptly ignored. Janice Hallquist, a friend and a great yoga teacher, has helped me keep my body limber over the years, allowing me to run with reduced risk to injury. Eva Solomon, an epic races director and tri-athlete, made timely editing suggestions for the book—and even cooler, designed my T-shirt for my 100th marathon in Boston. Melissa Sunderman, an elite tri-athlete, co-designed the shirt, and has been unrelenting in pushing the workout bar ever higher. Paula O'Brien is a dear friend, and she promised she would run her first marathon after reading *Let's Pick It Up a Bit*. Ellie Serras has shown me that it is never too late to run a marathon. Julie Parrish has been an inspiration as she's persisted in her journey to be a world-class athlete, despite many injuries. Gay MacGregor pushed me to start writing *Let's Pick It Up a Bit* in the first place. Jim Coleman encouraged me to run the Big Sur Marathon, a race I swore I would never run again. He made up for it by providing me valuable feedback for the book. Fazi "Dr. Nick" Nicklah is quite simply the most genteel person I have known. Sara Kazan takes a mean cover photo. And Randy Step, founder of Running Fit, has been a huge inspiration to me and the entire Midwest running community by organizing epic races like "Dances with Dirt" and encouraging us to have fun and not take ourselves too seriously.

Lastly, my colleagues, staff and patients at Enspire Dental and *The Dental Advisor* have been a crucial part of my adventures for the past thirty-one years. Their questions, interest and energy have kept me motivated and young.

This book is written to all past, present and future runners. Remember to run with passion—you'll feel great when you're done. Trust me.

The Breakfast Club
Back row L–R: Ron Yapp, Heinz Grassl, Ted Beimel, Tony Sullivan, John Powers

Front row L–R: Bob Marty, Nelson, John, Stan Watson

About the Authors

▼ ▼ ▼ ▼ ▼ ▼ ▼

John Farah

John Farah ran his very first race at the age of twelve—a 200-yard dash as a Boy Scout in Nazareth. Since then, he has run 416 more, including 121 marathons, 57 half-marathons, and 102 10Ks, logging over 80,000 miles of running. Not to mention seventeen Boston Marathons, a feat of which he's particularly proud. A passionate proponent of fitness and health, John currently lives with his wife Jackie, in Ann Arbor, Michigan, where he's had a successful dental practice for the last thirty years.

Nelson Williams

Nelson Williams ran his first race, a 600-yard run, at age thirteen, and then went on to become a sprinter in high school. His first distance race, an eight-miler, occurred more than ten years later, and happened only after relentless prodding from his brother Bruce. Nelson has always preferred the shorter races, but he has still completed twenty marathons—eighteen since he met John Farah. Nelson, who also loves long-distance bicycle trips, lives in Saline, Michigan, with his wife Corinne, and four Nova Scotia Duck-Tolling Retrievers. He worked for thirty-five years as an engineer in the auto industry before retiring in 2008.

Christopher Farah

Christopher Farah is a screenwriter and filmmaker living in Los Angeles, California. His first movie, "Answer This," is available on DVD at www.answerthismovie.com.